Love! Laugh! Panic!
Life with My Mother

By Rosemary Mild

Magic Island Literary Works   Honolulu, Hawaii   2014

Copyright © 2014 by Rosemary Mild
Printed in the United States of America by **Magic Island Literary Works.**

All rights reserved. No part of this book may be reproduced in any manner whatsoever without written permission except in the case of brief quotations embodied in critical articles and reviews. For further information please contact the publishers at:
<u>roselarry@magicile.com</u>

Cover design by Marilyn Drea Mac-In-Town.
Interior book design by Larry Mild.

Library of Congress Cataloging-in-Publication Data
Mild, Rosemary P.
Love! Laugh! Panic! Life with My Mother
Mild, Rosemary P.
ISBN 978-0-9838597-7-2

"I Learned From My Husband" by Luby Pollack: Originally published in the January 1945 *Parents*®Magazine. Reprinted by permission.

"The Good Deed Man" by Luby Pollack originally appeared in the *Wisconsin Jewish Chronicle*, May 7 and May 14, 1948. Reprinted by permission.

"Goodbye, Dolly" was originally published in a different form in *Washington Parent*, January/February, 1997.

The photograph of Grandma and Grandpa Bragarnick appeared in the *Milwaukee Sentinel* on May 10, 1948. Reprinted by permission of the MILWAUKEE JOURNAL SENTINEL.

Front cover: Rosemary's mother, Luby Bragarnick, at age twenty.

First Edition 2014

10 9 8 7 6 5 4 3 2 1

For our daughters, Jackie and Myrna

For our beloved grandchildren—
Alena, Craig, Ben, Leah, and Emily

For Larry—my husband, my partner, my soul mate

*In loving memory of our daughter
Miriam Luby Wolfe, who was so much
like my mother in all the best ways.*

Acknowledgments

I am enormously grateful for all the help I received in writing this book. My thanks to:

My brother, John Pollack, for his recollections of his relationship to our mother. He also discovered, and shared with me, Father's scrapbook containing Mother's published articles.

My sister-in-law Ann Pollack, who read this manuscript with an eagle eye and gave me astute advice.

My cousin Sue Baumblatt, who contributed memorable stories and recipes.

The staff at the *Wisconsin Jewish Chronicle*, who helped me track down Mother's articles about Grandpa Harry. They pointed me to Jay Hyland, Archivist at the Jewish Museum Milwaukee. He actually located the two 1948 articles (even though I had the year wrong) and sent me copies.

Marilyn Drea, Mac-In-Town Graphic Design Services, Annapolis, Md. She always brings us her expertise and good nature.

LOVE! LAUGH! PANIC!
Life with My Mother

Contents

CHAPTER

      So Why Did I Write This Book? **viii**

1. Urgent! Send Money! **1**

2. Goodbye, Dolly **2**

3. Lies I Should Never Have Told **5**

4. Journalist and Author **13**

5. September Blaze **23**

6. Our Jewish Home **25**

7. Letters to My Family from Smith **28**

8. Memories from My Brother, John Pollack **31**

9. On Being a Bad Sister—Sometimes **38**

10. Aunt Lucy **44**

11. Together in the Kitchen—for Better or Worse **48**

12. Grandma Minnie and Grandpa Henry **56**

13. Grandma Elizabeth and Grandpa Harry **58**

14. The Good Deed Man **60**

15. "You Have Such a Pretty Face" **69**

16. The Debutante **90**

    Looking Back, A Photo Album **118**

So Why Did I Write This Book?

My parents didn't give me a middle name. When I asked my mother why, she told me "Rosemary" was long enough. But her reasoning left me disgruntled, as if an essential part of me were missing. At age fourteen, after reading *Gone with the Wind* and *Forever Amber*, I made a declaration at the dinner table.

"I've decided to give myself a middle name. My first choice is Scarlett, but I'll settle for Amber."

"Jewish girls aren't called Scarlett or Amber," Mother said. "Now clear the table, please."

Maybe she hoped I would fill in the missing name abstractly, by becoming the next Marie Curie or Anna Pavlova. I dreamed that I was destined for great things. "Things" have happened my whole life, but not always what I had in mind.

I grew up in Milwaukee, Wisconsin. My maiden name was Rosemary Pollack. My mother's maiden name was Luby Bragarnick. Interesting that she didn't have a middle name either. She married my father, Dr. Saul Kenneth Pollack.

I originally intended to publish a collection of my essays, *In My Next Life I'll Get It Right*. It will come eventually, but first in the form of my very own blog. I had four key essays done. But when I read them over, I realized they're not just about me. They're about Mother and me. Even though she doesn't play a large part in every scene, she's always there. Looming. Encouraging. Warning. Always the Protagonist, the Star, the Heroine, the Antagonist, and sometimes the Villain from the viewpoint of a loving but ornery daughter.

I'm also the daughter of a psychoanalyst, which makes me a

great believer in Free Association. This sometimes presents a problem for me in real life. Father called me a daydreamer, "a wool gatherer." I spend a lot of time fantasizing. Now this is both good and bad. Dr. Joyce Brothers once said that people typically spend at least 30 percent of their time fantasizing. It's "healthy," because it takes us out of our daily problems on a sort of mini-vacation. And we can visualize ourselves accomplishing fabulous things.

But the flip side is a comment I read in *Psychology Today*: that people who fantasize a lot accomplish less than people who just pragmatically get to it and "work work work work work" (to quote the delightfully crazed Mel Brooks in *Blazing Saddles*). I call them Action People. My husband, Larry, is one of them. He never visualizes himself up on a podium receiving the Pulitzer Prize for Literature or as the inventor of the ultimate electric car. He decides he's going to add shelves to a closet or write another novel and just does it. As our friend Sheila Litzky, who introduced us, once said, "Larry is the Energizer Bunny, but cuter."

At one point I intended to write an essay about my life at Smith College. Exclusively my life, a thousand miles from home, but I discovered that it still involved my relationship to Mother. I couldn't separate myself out. My Smith life interweaves like a tapestry with experiences, conversations, arguments, passions, and hatreds from other times and places.

So here I am. This book is a portrait of my amazing mother. It's also a journey into our family, adventures and misadventures. Strap on your parachute and come along.

Larry never knew my mother, but he and my father hit it off instantly. We memorialized my father as Dr. Avi Kepple in *Locks and Cream Cheese,* our first Paco and Molly mystery.

Oh, one more thing. Names with quote marks around them have been changed to protect identities.

Rosemary Mild
2014

Chapter 1

Urgent! Send Money!

In 1932, my parents, Luby and Saul Pollack, spent their honeymoon in London. My father had graduated from medical school and completed his residency in psychiatry. Afterward, he landed a position for several months of postgraduate work in neurology at Queens Hospital.

From London a telegram arrived in Milwaukee, Wisconsin, for Luby's parents, Harry and Elizabeth Bragarnick. "Urgent! Wire $500 immediately."

Imagine what $500 was worth in 1932. Harry and Elizabeth were panic-stricken. Their daughter had been frail and sickly during a great deal of her childhood. Had some terrible illness overtaken her? Did she need an operation?

When the honeymooners returned from London, the truth came out. Luby had spent the $500 on a custom-designed set of Royal Worcester china. Twelve place settings, plus soup bowls and salad plates, cups and saucers, large platters, and a gravy boat. The china was exquisite. White with a wide border of rich, deep blue. An elaborate pattern of gold loops danced through the border, decorated at intervals with tiny hand-painted orange dots. Yes, hand-painted.

Harry was furious, but his fury didn't last long. Luby was the favorite of his three daughters; she was the most like him, with an incisive mind and flamboyant, charismatic personality.

Chapter 2

Goodbye, Dolly

For my sixth birthday party, in the summer of 1941, my mother hired a horse with a man to lead us on rides around the neighborhood. Not a pony, mind you, but a tall, colossal horse. It was also on my sixth birthday that my parents gave me my first doll. Smiling and rubbery, with kinky yellow hair, it came tucked inside a beige wicker buggy. After my guests had gone home, I took my doll for a walk, contentedly pushing the buggy for blocks and blocks through our Milwaukee neighborhood, not having the slightest notion of where I was going, nor caring. The tree-shaded sidewalks were silent, and I was alone and happy in the world.

Suddenly, a police car pulled up beside me and a huge officer climbed out. "I'm Sergeant Henderson," he said. "Your mother sent me to bring you home." I couldn't figure out why. What had I done wrong? He gently piled me and my buggy into the back seat of his cruiser.

My parents were frantic because I had been gone for hours. "Go to your room!" Mother shouted. "Some gratitude for your birthday party!" This was not just Time Out. This was Year Out, Decade Out. It probably wasn't more than an hour, but from then on, I despised dolls and buggies.

Mother lavished riches on me because as a child she didn't have any. She arrived at Ellis Island from Russia when she was five with her sister and parents. In first grade, Mother had only one dress. It had a white collar and cuffs, which Grandma Elizabeth washed and ironed each night and sewed back on so little Luby would look clean for school.

Mother never had a doll, which explains why she lovingly bought me one for Chanukah when I was nine. I thanked her loudly, but grateful I wasn't. I had never gotten over the Sixth-Birthday Doll-Buggy Disaster.

This new doll was aristocratic, almost two feet tall, with porcelain body and face, shiny auburn locks, and blue eyes with curly black lashes. It came in its own wooden cradle and was so important to Mother that she even named it: Penelope. A name I hated. My doll lay there forlorn and unappreciated for two years until one day I picked it up. I was curious about the arms and legs, how well they'd move. Not well, I discovered. In the split second it took Penelope to bat her lashes at me, I twisted off her right leg. Was it a Freudian accident, a subconscious rebellion against my mother? I'll never know. Toys do get broken, more often than not.

But this little act of destruction terrified me. I couldn't just tell her the truth. So I laid Penelope back in her cradle and set the leg firmly in place so she'd look whole again. For the next three months, every time Mother came in my room I held my breath. I willed her not to notice. But of course one day she did—because the right leg was now a bit longer than the left. To my surprise, she didn't scold or yell.

"What happened?" she asked.

"I don't know," I whimpered.

Penelope meant so much to Mother that she carted her off to the doll hospital in downtown Milwaukee for hip replacement surgery, very successful, I'm happy to report. Nevertheless, I wasted no emotion over it.

Mother knew better than to ever buy me another doll. But she did make me one: a black yarn doll with a red yarn dress that you could take off and put on. Its eyes are embroidered in brown and its hair is arranged in tiny pigtails all over its head, secured in red yarn ribbons. Back then it was called a pickaninny doll—politically incorrect today, of course. Mother made it out of squares of yarn woven on a frame with little steel spikes. She let me make some of the squares, and I had a grand sense of accomplishment weaving the yarn in and out. She even taught me to finish off the squares so they wouldn't unravel.

Today the doll sits high on a shelf at home, one of my treasures: a symbol of my mother's love for me and her endless desire to make a place for dolls in my life.

Chapter 3

Lies I Should Never Have Told

Lying to my mother—and getting away with it—took skill. Early in life I honed it to a fine art. Or so I thought.

My parents had enormous aspirations for me, so they threw me into a smorgasbord of activities as if they were playing pickup sticks, hoping at least one of them would land free and clear and reflect some talent.

That's how I landed at Miss Parchel's for piano lessons. She taught in a time-worn mansion: red stone with a Romanesque arched façade and creaking plank floors—the perfect setting for her. Skinny, with worried eyes and crinkly hair, "Miss Parchel" looked like a spinster escaped from Jane Austen's quill pen. Her specialty was training musically gifted children to be concert pianists. Apparently, there weren't enough of them to sustain her in food and lodging, because she accepted me. I had no talent or even a desire to play, yet my parents doggedly wasted three dollars a week, starting in 1943. Maybe they felt sorry for her.

But I didn't complain because the lessons turned into a thrill that had nothing to do with the piano. That's where I met dashing, dark-haired Tommy Brown, who laughed easily and loved mischief as much as music. In my eight-year-old's eyes, he was an older man, all of ten. Between our lessons, we'd dash outside and chase each other, tearing around the mansion through the weedy grass. Now *he* was a gifted pianist. His father played first-chair violin with the Milwaukee Symphony Orchestra. At Miss Parchel's recitals, she always placed Tommy last, and he always performed brilliantly.

I was supposed to practice an hour a day, including a loooooong medley of scales. Instead, my sessions consisted of building a credible lie without sitting down at the piano. If Mother happened to be out of the house after school, I'd report: "I practiced from 3:15 to 3:45 and 4:05 to 4:35." This deception went on for six years, but it didn't fool either my mother or father, because I never improved. At my last recital, Miss Parchel assigned me an etude so short that if you sneezed you missed it.

My parents finally let me off the hook. And that's when our family made an astonishing discovery. My eleven-year-old brother became a terrific jazz pianist—without a single lesson.

* * *

We had a sometime cleaning lady, an older woman with a heavy body, too heavy for floor washing. Mother was out. After Mrs. Frenzen left for the day I decided to help out by washing the kitchen floor on my own. I was ten. We had a squeegee and a small wooden frame that fit over the bucket. You pushed the squeegee down on the wooden piece to ooze the water out of it. I pushed down so hard that the wooden piece broke. Horrified, I took it down the basement and hid it under the bucket in the laundry room. And, of course, said nothing to Mother. The next time she went to get out the floor-washing equipment there was the broken piece. Mother was so mad she called Mrs. Frenzen, who rightfully denied knowing anything about it. Finally, after agonizing hours, Mother realized I was the criminal. "Why didn't you tell me?" she demanded. I couldn't say a word. I just cried.

The point is this. It was all part of the feeling that I had to succeed in anything I did. I couldn't admit being wrong or making mistakes. The bigger issue, though, is why Mother made such a huge deal out of a lousy little piece of broken wood. And embarrassed the hapless cleaning lady. Obsessive, no matter what the cost.

* * *

Love! Laugh! Panic!

The cigarette tasted horrible. But I didn't care. I was sixteen and had discovered Kents—long, sexy, filtered—at a party after one of our high school football games. My goal was to look sophisticated, and for that to happen, I had to learn to inhale. So there I was at midnight, seated at my dressing table, studying my progress in the mirror as I puffed away. I was just getting the hang of it when I heard the door to my parents' room open and a pad-pad-padding down the hall.

Oh, boy! I set the ashtray on the floor, with the lit cigarette in it, and shoved it under the dressing table. Surely, the flowered chintz skirt would hide my crime.

No polite knock. In burst Mother in her nightgown and bare feet. "Rosemary, stop smoking this instant!"

"I'm not!"

"Don't lie to me. I can see the smoke pouring out of the dressing table. You're going to start a fire. And you're filling the whole house up with smoke!"

That was the last time I ever smoked in my room—or even in the house. But it wasn't my last cigarette. Far from it. For years I basked in the dubious joys of smoking. Tobacco breath carried its own special penalties. Shortly after high school graduation, I had a date with a tall, stunning boy from temple in my Junior Congregation class. I'd wanted to go out with him for a long time. At my house after a movie, we were dancing in the living room when he complained, "How come you always keep your head down? You never look up at me?" I was too embarrassed and ashamed to tell him the truth: my cigarette breath smelled stale and rancid. He never called me again.

Theater intermissions meant desperately stumbling over knees and feet to get out to the lobby to smoke. Freshman year at Smith I took cigarette breaks in The Smoker, the only place in the dorm where we were allowed to smoke. One late night only one other girl was there. She sat down beside me and said, "Rosemary, you have beautiful lips." "Thank you," I said mechanically, having never been faced with such an alarming compliment. I sprang up and fled to my room—and never entered The Smoker again unless there was a whole flock of girls there.

Severe chest pains propelled me to a pulmonary specialist for an x-ray. Did I have lung cancer? I didn't, but then a new wrinkle started. When I bent down to pick up something off the floor, my leg bones creaked with a hollow sound. Something bad was going on. By the time I was twenty-three, I was smoking a pack a day—all of it after work, hating the taste, hating the yellow stains on my fingers. Still I kept puffing away. But who was I kidding? If only I had listened to Mother. After eight years and six attempts, I finally quit for good. It took three years for the chest pains to disappear.

* * *

If there had been a Nobel Prize for Hiding the Truth from One's Parents, I'd have won it. Freshman year at Smith, Mother visited me one raw Massachusetts day in November. It was brave of her to come alone. Two airplanes and a cab ride from Milwaukee to my isolated Victorian college town of Northampton in the Berkshires.

We sat on my bed in my room. It wasn't easy for her to walk up the four flights, but she did. "Tell me how school's going. How are your classes? How are your grades?"

"Oh, great!" I gushed. "No problem at all. I'm handling the work just fine."

She ate dinner with me and my friends in the genteel dining room. I chewed my pot roast slowly as Mother cheerfully dominated the conversation. She asked the girls about themselves, where they were from, what they were majoring in. And she raved about the zebra, the loaf of chocolate wafers layered with whipped cream and sliced on a slant. So I didn't have to talk much. That made it easy not to spill the details and confess the truth about my crisis that very morning.

In Religion 11, the professor had handed back our first midterm. I stared at my grade: a screaming red D. I couldn't believe it. I was Jewish. The first six weeks were on Judaism! Humiliation total. A note scrawled under the grade issued an order. "See me in my office after class."

"Let me see your notebook," the professor demanded.

Meekly, I slid it toward her. Her eyes scanned the pages, then glared at me from behind granny glasses. "You don't know how to study."

Her blunt, raspy voice boxed my ears. *I don't? How could this be? I came from one of the best high schools in Wisconsin. Got high grades. Got into Smith.*

With military precision, she issued orders. "Here's what you need to do. Read the textbook. Take notes. Write down the title of the textbook and the page numbers in the left margin of your notebook, so you know where you got the material. When you study for a test, go over your lecture notes *and* text notes." She glanced at me slyly. "Maybe you were relying too much on material you *thought* you remembered from Sunday School."

Ouch! Exactly! I slunk out, climbed on my second-hand bike, and pedaled back to the Quad. I didn't breathe a word to Mother during her visit. I didn't have to. On my first report card, which the college mailed directly to parents, I got a C in Religion 11. The Judaism grade did it.

* * *

At times, Mother and I actually became co-conspirators. Even when I was in junior high, she often trusted me, like when she bought a new hat, plushy pink with matching spangles. "It cost $40," she whispered. "Don't tell your father."

The hat also served as a ruse. My parents were going out for the evening with their best friends. Mother was always late. Father, already dressed, was pacing the living room waiting for her. The Allens arrived to pick them up, idling the engine in front of the house. Mother plopped the pink hat on her head and leaned out the master bedroom second-floor window. "I'll be right down," she called.

From my perch on the bed I giggled. Typical Mother—still in her slip. And the Allens always knew it.

Before a party, Mother would assign me to clean the house—including my parents' room. That was shorthand for making everything disappear. I expertly gathered up all the clothes, shoes, jewelry, books, and magazines, and stuffed them under the bed or in the closet. But the best-laid plans . . .

Our first night on vacation in the Wisconsin Dells, my parents got a phone call from the Whitefish Bay Police. Back then you left a key with the police and an officer would check on your house while you were away. "Your bedroom has been ransacked, Doctor," he told my father. "Stockings and stuff hanging out of drawers, clothes on the floor." Father groaned, placed his hand over the receiver, and told Mother. She flushed, tittered with embarrassment, and confessed: "Never mind." That was how she'd left the room.

We never got to grow old together, Mother and I. She died at age forty-eight of a rare form of stomach cancer. But the closeness we shared, whether lies or conspiracies, remain snuggled in my heart.

Mother's book publicity photo—in her Paris suit.

The press release for her book speeches.

Chapter 4

Journalist and Author

I wish I had spent more time learning from Mother instead of resenting, ignoring, or fearing her.

Luby Bragarnick graduated from the University of Wisconsin as a journalism major in 1929. She immediately landed a job as an advertising copywriter at the Boston Store, a major Milwaukee department store. The job didn't last long. She was caught at her desk making up her wedding guest list. Fired on the spot, Mother resolved to never again work for someone else.

She became a free-lance writer, publishing under her married name, Luby Pollack, in the *Milwaukee Journal, Collier's, Parents* ® Magazine, *The American Home, Wisconsin Jewish Chronicle, Today's Health*, and elsewhere.

Finally, she authored a book that became a Milwaukee bestseller: *Your Normal Mind: Its Tricks and Quirks.* Here's one of my favorite excerpts, from her chapter "Remarkable Coincidences."

One Thursday afternoon in January my younger sister's husband, a lawyer, let himself into his house in Washington, D.C. His wife hurried to greet him. She said: 'I could hardly wait till you got here. I've been smelling smoke for hours, and I've hunted all over the house, and can't find where it comes from.' My brother-in-law immediately started searching the house—upstairs and down, in attic and basement and in every spot where a fire could smolder surreptitiously; he had had engineer training, and therefore had a better than common knowledge of the mechanical appliances that could misbehave. But he found nothing wrong anywhere. Finally he reported that if anything was burning, it was probably the roast beef, and how about dinner?

That night my sister slept badly. Friday morning the acrid smell of smoke was still in her nostrils, and she felt unaccountably distressed. Here is the coincidence. It was six o'clock Eastern Standard Time when my brother-in-law was inspecting his house in Washington. At that hour—five o'clock Central Standard Time—a fire was smoldering in the basement walls of my house in Milwaukee. Was it mere coincidence?

No. It was in this chapter that Mother introduced the phenomenon ESP: extrasensory perception.

Kids don't always "get" who their parents really are. I was so busy being a teenager that I didn't fully comprehend her accomplishment. The book came out in 1949, when I was fourteen. In 2012 I was able to order it on Amazon—a used copy of the edition published in England. Rereading it today, I'm astonished at Mother's intellectual prowess, delivered in crisp, friendly style. Her acknowledgments include the Medical Library of Marquette University. Her index of references and quotes spans five pages. In addition to ESP, her chapters deal with such phenomena as hallucinations, clairvoyance, *déjà vu*, unconscious motivation, hypnosis, and the death wish.

Usually a charismatic speaker, Mother gave book talks. Her promotional flyer described her two speeches. One was on the trials and tribulations of juggling roles as an author, wife of a psychoanalyst, and mother of two teenagers. Her other speech dealt with the meat of the book itself. One of her most important talks was for a large temple Sisterhood in Chicago, a sophisticated audience. Around suppertime, Father, John, and I met her train. As she stepped down in her stunning Paris suit and velvet beret, she didn't look herself. Tears poured down her rouged cheeks. Mother did not cry easily. Her first words to us, before she had even set both feet on the platform, were: "I gave the wrong speech." What happened? She chose the one with the funny anecdotes, which charmed Milwaukee audiences, because they all knew the four of us personally or were Father's patients. But in Chicago, nobody knew us. Not a single woman in the audience laughed or warmed to Mother's words. She had not yet learned how to shift gears, to gauge an audience.

One could hardly ignore the fact that she wrote a book

touching on her own husband's field of expertise. My father was a pioneer in psychiatry and psychoanalysis in the state of Wisconsin. Why did his wife choose this subject? She was a highly competitive, driven woman. Was she competing with him? Trying to beat him at his own game? I don't think so. I think her aim was to bring an understanding of mental phenomena, the workings of the human brain, closer to the average person on the street. In her acknowledgments she wrote: "And to my husband, who sat in such constantly severe judgment." He was her master critic, pointing her toward his colleagues and other experts she needed to consult; the relevant books by Sigmund Freud and other authors; and anecdotes from his own practice. Father guided her to be the best she could be.

As a free-lance feature writer, Mother found subjects everywhere. We had an Italian produce man, Sam Fricano, who came once a week in his boxy white truck and delivered sumptuous fruits and vegetables to us at the back door. Mother started chatting with him about his business, his wife, and her cooking. Sam invited her to a home-cooked meal. Thus began an entire series on ethnic cooking: Italian, Chinese, Greek, Czech, Jewish, Mexican, Russian, and a southern meal at Babe's Barbecue—with Mother as personal guest. The series appeared in the *Milwaukee Journal* feature section, the Green Sheet.

One summer she and Father drove up north to visit John and me at our two camps. They stopped at a chicken farm for lunch and met a woman there with an unusual profession: Doris the Chicken Doctor, whose national expertise began on the family farm at age nine. Mother's article, "The Little Doc," appeared in *Collier's*, biggest rival of the *Saturday Evening Post*.

"Oh Glamorous Washroom!" appeared in the February 1944 issue of *American Home* and later in the magazine's booklet *Paint It Up*. Mother despised our drab, tiny guest bathroom. She had no experience as a decorator or artist, but that didn't stop her. She happened upon four framed pictures of camellias and used them as a theme. The outside of the powder room door welcomed guests to The Camellia House. After painting the walls a soft pink, she traced the flowers and lavishly embellished them on the walls. Just below the ceiling, she scripted a quotation from "Elegy in a Country Churchyard" by eighteenth-century poet Thomas Gray:

"Full many a flower is born to blush unseen and waste its sweetness on the desert air."

Then Mother turned around and wrote what I call a self-exposé. It was originally published in the January 1945 *Parents* ® Magazine. It was also dramatized in a radio show called *Parents* ® *Magazine on the Air*.

"I Learned From My Husband"

This four-year-old's mother called it "stealing" but her spankings didn't help. Nothing did till she tried her husband's plan.

By LUBY POLLACK

After the shrieking had subsided and John was crying softly in his room, my husband turned to me and asked:

"All right. What did you gain by it?"

My half-spent anger flared up again. Shaking my finger in his face I exploded a second time.

"I'll tell you what I gained. I'm all through with hanky-pank psychology, Wise Man. From now on when John steals my watch or my bracelet, or even a toothpick, he's going to get spanked. I'll spank and spank and keep right on spanking, until he learns that no child in this house will be a thief. No more cajoling, no more reasoning. I'm all through with that nonsense."

For a moment my husband considered this violent speech, then he said, "If you're going to resort to beating—"

"Beating!" I protested. "Don't be a goon."

"O.K. Call it spanking if it makes you any happier. But if that's your way of handling a tough problem, please don't expect any help from me. For I say the child is not stealing. He's only four. What does a four-year-old know of the sanctity of property? Your watch intrigues him; he wants to see what makes it go. Is that bad? Do you think you can teach him to respect other people's things by the hit-hard-and-hope method?"

But I was not listening to my husband, who by the way is a psychiatrist. For months I had been harassed and worried by John's tendency to take things out of dresser drawers, cupboards and tool chests. I had tried to explain and in his big-eyed way John had seemed to understand. "No more stealing, Mommy," he had invariably answered. But two days later something else would be tucked away in his snow-suit pocket or hidden in his wheelbarrow, to be explored outside where I couldn't see.

It had been a wrist watch, a billfold with trick pockets, an enameled music box, a silver teapot. But this time I had reached the end of my rope. This time it had been the watch that we had found in Zurich. My husband and I both cherished it and all of the lovely memories it evoked. My answer to John had been a sound spanking.

It wasn't that I hadn't tried to reason with my son.

"You see," I had said, "Wouldn't it be queer if people came into our house and took whatever they liked?"

Once I resorted to tears. "Please, Johnny, don't hurt Mother by taking things that don't belong to you." To my credit let me admit that I was ashamed of this emotional approach.

Nothing seemed to have helped. John continued to take things, surreptitiously, and sometimes they were broken or bent. Each time I knew the monstrous fear that my child would grow up without moral or ethical code.

It is my husband's business, as a psychiatrist, to help human beings meet their problems, but for the first time in our eleven years of marriage I had completely lost faith in the psychological approach. Whack 'em and whack 'em good was my new creed. Small John felt the impact of my hand frequently in the following weeks.

A curious thing began to happen. John didn't like me to read to him any more. When he left for kindergarten he turned his face away from my kiss. He preferred to play at other children's homes. Even the enticing offer of a cocoa party where he could be Mr. Jones-come-to-call had lost its enchantment. The question of his bath became a tug of war. "I'll wait for Daddy," was his stubborn dictum.

He found little ways to annoy me. When I talked on the phone he'd chant a poem loud enough to make it difficult for me to hear; as soon as I was finished he was too. At dinner he would eye the corn avidly, because he loved corn, but when I'd say, "I fixed the corn especially for you, son," he'd push it aside. "I don't care for any corn, thank you."

And the "stealing" continued.

One evening I timidly broached the subject to my

husband again. Timidly, because I suspected my tactics had failed. The "stealing" was done as before, undiminished in frequency, and I had only succeeded in adding a second problem—the problem of my boy's antagonism toward me.

My husband was matter-of-fact. "I don't want to be mean about this," he said, "but you chose the spankings. I have nothing to offer."

Pride and hurt rode the crest for another few weeks until I finally humbled myself. I telephoned my husband's office, and made an appointment to see him.

I sat in the waiting room, took my turn, until I was ushered in.

I told him the story of John from beginning to end as if I were a complete stranger. My side of the story, the "thefts," the spankings, the resentment. He listened as objectively as if he had never seen me before.

The plan my husband laid out was this. Once a day, whenever it was convenient for me, I was to give John permission to take out the entire jewel tray from my dresser. Lay out all the pins and necklaces, the earrings, bracelets and watches. Play jewelry store man with everything—but carefully because he was a storekeeper who treasured his costly wares. Then after John had had his fill of play he was to put each piece back as it was, and close his shop for the day.

Never in my years as a mother have I seen such joy in a child's face as I saw in John's when this play plan was suggested. Never did I believe that rough-tough little John could handle things so gently, so lovingly.

The success of the scheme transcended even my hopes. We carried it further, to Daddy's tool chest, to the kettle cupboard, and my writing desk. Each time John was a different kind of storekeeper, a hardware man, a pot vendor, a stationery seller. John was having a beautiful time.

For three months John has not touched a single possession that is not strictly his own.

One day in jest I asked my husband for a bill "for services rendered."

"You bet you're going to pay me for services rendered," he said. "You're going to pay me with promises."

"Promises," I echoed. "What kind of promises?"

"Promises," he repeated, "that you'll discipline yourself before you discipline John.

"First, when John asks to play with something that's yours or mine, promise that you won't brush him off with an impatient 'no.' Remember he's a small child with small thinking. He doesn't understand, for instance, that your precious china balloon man is Royal Doulton. To him it's only a swell toy. Certainly he shouldn't play with it, but accord him the respect due him by considering his request seriously. Prove that you want to be fair. Let him hold it a minute, and explain how it was made, and why it is so valuable."

That didn't seem too difficult.

"This one is much tougher but, believe me, it's more important than you've wanted to realize," my husband said. "Suppose John does break something. Don't rush at him like an avenging angel. Be calm. Ask questions quietly. Find out if the damage was intentional or accidental. Find out whether he has deliberately trespassed in forbidden areas.

"If you are calm, your judgment is pretty certain to be more sound. If you do decide to punish him, at least he'll know that you gave him an honest and reasonable hearing first."

#

Which brings me to my first-grade teacher, "Miss Rothberg." One of my classmates was a gangly farm boy who wore highcuts, tall boots with silver hooks to hold the laces. Carl was a bit slow with the correct answers, and seemed to bring out the worst in Miss Rothberg. She scolded him a lot. I still remember feeling sad for him and resenting the teacher for embarrassing him. Only recently did I figure out why these scenes have nagged at me for seventy years. It wasn't so much Miss Rothberg who disturbed me. It was my own mother, for being too hard on John. Now why was this?

John is three-and-a-half years younger than I. He was a preemie, born six weeks early, on Thanksgiving Day. When it was time for him to start school, my parents had a huge decision to make. Born on November 25, he would no doubt be the youngest child in his class. Should they hold him back a year so he could grow up a bit? They knew he was a bright little boy, so they chose to plunge him into school his own year.

It's a well-known fact that often little girls mature faster than boys in the beginning. They generally have longer attention spans and more dexterous small motor skills. I was a fast learner, and we had an impatient mother. Interesting that she had infinite patience for getting her journalism right, but little patience for John, who took longer than I to get his homework done. By junior high John had turned into a brainy kid, eventually carving out a fine profession as a mechanical engineer, complete with a master's degree.

John grew strong and stocky as a teenager. Mother had several levels of annoyance for him. At age seven if he whined she called him "Eeyore." When he was fourteen and she potched him on the rear end, he just stood there and crowed with delight. Mother stood there rubbing her skinny wrist.

Her levels of annoyance with me—now that was a different story.

The thing I remember most about Mother and her writing is this. She was physically frail, with stomach trouble her whole life. The editor of the *Wisconsin Jewish Chronicle* wrote her: "I would like to have you do a series of articles on various local community institutions such as the Home for the Aged . . . I would also like you to consider accepting a permanent position on the Chronicle staff as feature writer." Mother's reply: "This letter is being written to you just one hour before I leave my home to go to Chicago. I will be admitted to Presbyterian Hospital tonight, and tomorrow morning I am undergoing surgery."

Mentally she was strong, tough, powerfully determined. Sometimes she'd wake up at 2 a.m., run down the stairs barefoot, and type out a new idea on her Smith Corona manual typewriter. Of course, manual. There was no other kind back then.

And speaking of typewriters . . . I finished sixth grade a month before my twelfth birthday, with one glorious week to play and do whatever I wanted before going off to camp.

My first morning of freedom, at 7 a.m., Mother charged into the room. "Get up! You're going to learn to type."

"No I'm not."

"Yes you are. Get up!"

She walked me to the high school three blocks away, a huge, scary Gothic structure, and marched me into the summer school typing class. There were thirty of us. I was the only elementary school child. Everyone else was a high school student.

Six days later, I had learned to touch-type. The class continued for the rest of the session without me. I went off to Camp Pinemere in the Wisconsin North Woods. One afternoon the mother of one of my cabinmates came to visit. Sitting on my cot, I announced to her: "I'm practicing my typing."

"What do you mean?" she asked. "You don't have a typewriter."

"I do it with my fingers on my knees," I said.

The mother walked away. I didn't know a kid my age could spook a mother.

Six years later, I was co-editor-in-chief of the *Tower Times* at Whitefish Bay High. I was typing an article when our journalism adviser happened to walk by. She stopped behind my chair and cleared her throat. "Rosemary, you're typing G's and H's with your thumbs."

"What's wrong with that?" I asked.

"You're supposed to use your index fingers."

"Oh." During my six days in the class, the summer typing teacher never got around to checking my work. I must have appeared invisible among all the big kids.

That class may have been the best thing Mother ever did for me. But sometimes she overdid. In ninth grade we had to write our autobiography. Mine was sixty-six handwritten pages, and Mother offered to type it for me. Naturally, I trusted her and didn't look at the typed copy until the night before it was due. To my horror, I discovered she hadn't just typed it; she had rewritten it. With no time left to copy my version by hand, I turned it in and received an A+. I didn't dare tell the teacher the truth, but I felt like I had cheated.

So why did she rewrite my autobiography? In a way she couldn't help herself. Her drive to succeed was so overwhelming, so compulsive, that she had to interfere and push me.

A feeling of dread began to pile up inside me, like garbage

accumulating at the city dump. Mother's list of negatives about her daughter was growing. I was too fat. I wore glasses. And I wasn't a good writer.

Chapter 5

September Blaze

No, it wasn't a bonfire. It was the official name of the golden retriever puppy my parents bought John during that month when he was eleven. Shortly after, Blaze was diagnosed with Huntington's chorea, a fatal disease. The veterinarian could do nothing. Refusing to accept this diagnosis of doom, Father called his colleague to come over for a consultation. Dr. William Studley had been Father's roommate and best friend at Rush Medical College in Chicago. Now he owned a sanitarium a few miles from us.

Father placed Blaze on the kitchen table. Mother, John, and I hovered about, wringing our hands and sobbing. The two psychiatrists talked for a long time. Their decision was to ply Blaze with all the neurological drugs they thought might work. They saved his life. Blaze not only survived, he became strong. He had one side effect throughout his life: a tic that affected his whole body, including his head, even while he slept. Still, it never bothered him. Vigorous and lovable, he looked like he was always smiling and lived to age twelve.

At ten months old, Blaze had grown into an obstreperous hulk, as golden puppies do. He was so happy to see Aunt Lucy come in the front door that he leaped up and knocked her down on the sofa. When we took him to her house, John had to cover the dog's paws with baby booties before Lucy would allow him in. Uncle Maury made up a special name for him: Hullamoizer.

Blaze slept under the buffet. We did not have a dog bed. New wall-to-wall carpeting, pearl gray, had just been installed throughout our entire house. In the dining room stood the regal buffet on tall legs. One night about 2 a.m. our family woke up to a rumbling, churning noise. Half asleep, we all bumbled downstairs. There was Blaze, pawing away as if he were digging a hole in the backyard to bury a bone. And that's exactly what he was doing under the buffet. Creating a huge hole in the new carpet.

Mother shrieked, "He goes or I go!"

John and I trooped miserably back to bed. Would Mother follow through on her threat? A week later, the dog was still with us, but at seven o'clock at night, he darted out the front door and ran away. The four of us scoured the neighborhood, calling his name. No Blaze. We all went to bed, John and I in tears. About 4 a.m. Mother awoke with a start. She thought she heard a chain rattling. She ran downstairs, turned on the front porch light and all the living room lamps, and opened the front door. There stood Blaze, panting and grimy, wagging his tail and wiggling his huge body past her into the house.

So much for "He goes or I go."

During the fifteen months Mother was dying of cancer, confined to bed a great deal of the time, she couldn't tolerate the pungent breath that goldens are notorious for. So Blaze lay as close as he was allowed, all day long just outside the bedroom door.

Chapter 6

Our Jewish Home

We were quite Jewish. Both sets of grandparents were Orthodox. My father was the youngest of five boys and, as a child, little Saul had two special responsibilities. Every Friday he polished the sterling silver *Shabbat* candlesticks. And at Passover, he grated the fresh horseradish root, the *moror*—symbol of the Israelites' bitter lives under Egyptian slavery. During Rosh Hashanah Mother once took me to the small synagogue on Milwaukee's North Side where Grandpa Harry and Grandma Elizabeth and Grandpa Henry and Grandma Minnie worshiped. We sat upstairs, as all females had to. Looking down into the sanctuary, I saw Grandpa Harry, distinguished in his *tallis* and tall hat, reveling in the joy of the High Holy Days, shaking hands with his compatriots.

Passover was always held at Grandpa Harry and Grandma Elizabeth's, in their spacious apartment over their hosiery store. Under a crystal chandelier, we sat around the mahogany dining room table; it held all nineteen of us, including our families from Washington, D.C. and New York. We seven grandchildren fidgeted through the lengthy Seder, then stuffed on the cherry varnishkes and other delicious foods, not including gefilte fish, which was definitely a taste we had not yet acquired. But afterward, the long table was deserted, except for Grandpa Harry at one end and Grandpa Henry at the other, wearing their hats, finishing the service that the rest of us had abandoned. We had already found the *afikoman* and received our rewards. Our mothers were doing dishes; our fathers had escaped into the living room to chat; and we grandchildren ran around boisterously, glad to be liberated from the ritual.

John and I attended Sunday School at our reform synagogue every week, usually taking the bus to Temple Emanu-El B'ne Jeshurun in Milwaukee. Back then there was no Hebrew taught, no *bar* or *bat mizvahs*. But we did have Confirmation, and after Confirmation, Junior Congregation. I sang in the choir for the High Holy Days, in the choir loft, high above the bema, in English. Mother bought me a special dress, striped taffeta, with a pink rose at the waist.

My third-grade teacher was Miss Sweet, and she was! Also statuesque, pretty, and Jewish. Mother invited her to dinner, plus another guest: a Jewish, single Air Force major. Bingo! The matchmaking worked. They got married and had lots of children.

Mother belonged to Hadassah and ORT, an acronym for the Russian Society for Trades and Agricultural Labor. In the late 1800s, Jews in Russia created the society to help Jews—millions of whom were impoverished—learn trades and farming. It's a successful worldwide organization today.

We lit the Chanukah candles every night, and, of course, we had *latkes*, the fried potato pancakes. My job was to grate the peeled potatoes by hand. When I didn't grate fast enough, the raw shreds, exposed to the air, started to turn purple.

A couple years ago, the only time I ever watched the TV cartoon *Rug Rats*, I caught two old Jewish men arguing. One complained, "Latkes aren't good for you." His friend retorted, "We Jews have been clogging our arteries for two thousand years. Why stop now?"

But Mother had this thing: she also loved Christmas decorations. She was artistic and aesthetic, and appreciated their beauty. Nothing religious. So she brought home an armful of pine branches and created a centerpiece on the dining room table, plus another spray on the mantel in the living room. And added Christmas tree ornaments, shiny balls in red, gold, green, and silver. For some reason, this ambivalence did not strike us as odd. If Mother did it, it had to be right. Father merely tolerated it. But that wasn't all she did. She hung up Chanukah stockings for us on the mantel. They couldn't be called Christmas stockings because Mother used her own nylons. They were quite ludicrous and wonderful. Every time she tucked another small gift into them, they stretched—longer and longer, until the toes just about reached the floor. Our favorite surprise was marzipan: ground-almond sweets like miniature fruits: bananas, apples, plums, packed in tiny square wood boxes, replicas of those brought to market by farmers.

The most important Chanukah gift I ever received came when I was fourteen. After we'd lit the candles on the eighth night, Mother handed John and me each a copy of a huge, heavy book: *The Lincoln Library of Essential Information*. The two of us laughed, thinking this was a really funny present. But I didn't laugh long. It was a one-volume encyclopedia that became the mainstay of all my research in high school and college. Most touching of all, it was Mother's legacy, her dedication to and love of research.

Chapter 7

Letters to My Family from Smith

My grades at Smith were lousy. I only made Dean's List one semester in the entire four years.

I recently discovered, deep in a file cabinet, a packet of letters bound up in gray thread, with a note on top in Mother's graceful handwriting: "Rosemary's Freshman Year at Smith." She had saved all thirty-eight letters. I was flabbergasted that she had saved them. And now I know at least one reason why I got poor grades. I spent too much time writing to my family. Single-spaced, two and three pages, on Mother's manual Royal Portable. Think of all the good grades I could have gotten if I'd been studying more. But I thought I *was* studying more. Smith was so hard! So many brilliant girls!

After Thanksgiving weekend in New York, 1953, I wrote a huge letter filled with boys, boys, boys. College boys my friends and I met and bumped into, literally, in the crush Under the Clock at the Biltmore. That was supposed to be The Thing To Do. Quite pointless, really. We stayed at the Roosevelt, six of us in one room; it was all we could afford, and we attended a midnight jazz concert at Carnegie Hall. Here are a few of my letters.

Dear Family: . . . Friday Sue and I went shopping on Fifth Avenue and saw a fashion show at Lord & Taylor climaxed by Mrs. Anne Fogarty. Remember her, Mother? The designer who made my Oxford gray dress? Mrs. Anne Fogarty is a household word around Smith—she's extremely famous. She looked petite and lovely and led a toy gray French poodle on a leash. She pirouetted on the platform and then TRIPPED off. It was really funny. . . .

February '54. Second semester of freshman year:

Dear Family: I still don't know how I did on my paper on James Joyce for English. I've been warned not to expect an A. Upperclassmen say that even if you deserve it, the teacher never gives you the benefit of the doubt for the semester. Marks carry over and your average doesn't count till the end of the year. So they give you the lower grade to keep you working like a slave.

All the girls are taking turns getting into—pardon, Mother, but it's very descriptive—bitchy moods. My turn hasn't come yet, and by God, it's not going to. Sometimes, Mother, I lose complete patience and then I have to get on my bike and pedal up the biggest hill to get it all out of me. Polly was nasty to me for a week, so I avoided her and now she's all right again, so we're fine friends. Roxy changes moods every half-day, and Nicky is completely unpredictable. She told me this morning she hated Smith for all she was worth. Not because of me, though. I certainly haven't done a thing to bring that on. But since this is her first experience away from home, I must "be charitable and tolerant," unquote Mother. Lenore and I keep each other going. I'm positive she's one of the few freshmen in this house who are completely stable and well-adjusted. However, I've been feeling fine in spite of the morbid attitude of everyone since exams started. I refuse to get poisoned by the bitterness of girls who are dissatisfied, and believe me, Mother, there are plenty. Ever since Christmas vacation many of the girls dislike this place. Polly has applied for transfer to McGill. When I get home at springtime I'll tell you how these kids have changed. It's fascinating to observe, but Hell to put up with. I love this school, am getting every bit out of it that I wish and expect.

Reflecting on that letter five decades later, it was freshman exam panic that created the temporary monsters. Polly did transfer. And so did Roxy; at our fiftieth reunion, she confessed to me that she regretted leaving Smith. But oh, my God, in my letters, did I sound self-righteous! I recall saying to a friend, "I don't like your attitude"—about what I don't remember. Gee, one of my own monster moments. Being judgmental: that was a continuing problem of mine. Probably still is. I'm a little slow in breaking old habits.

April 21, 1954. Dear Family: Mother, thank you a million for the Hungarian butter-horns. Our housemother, Mrs. Fricke, was most amazed and simply thrilled with her package. We devoured ours in no time. They came on a weekend and on Sunday I passed them out to all the Yalies around (that I knew). They had never had them before and were very appreciative.

These rich, crescent-shaped pastries contain about a dozen ingredients and required at least twenty steps. I can't get over how energetic and kind Mother was to bake them for us. She sent them to me in two tins with the pastries cushioned in popcorn.

Hi Family! Whenever the food is bad at lunch we just leave the table. We're allowed to. (Not at dinner, which is more formal.) Today we had macaroni, bread, creamed onions, and rhubarb. Sunday nights we have buffet. The best thing about it is Desserts of the Week in Review.

I GOT AN A ON MY ENGLISH PAPER!!!!!!!!!!!!!!!!!!!!!!!!!!!!!! on "Riders to the Sea" by John Millington Synge.

I must admit, I'm getting a bit tired of everything. Boy, the constant push, push, push all year gets tedious and pressuring. Where have you heard this before? Every year since I began high school. The demands on us here are enormous. What I wouldn't do just for some sleep.

Love to my dear family and Animal. It's a shame Blaze doesn't do something heroic like Lassie and follow me all the way to Smith. Some dummy.

Chapter 8

Memories from My Brother, John Pollack

One of the first memories I have that delights me so much is about Mother and my photography hobby in high school. I developed my own 8 x 10 prints. One day I made a very nice family portrait and I was going to mount it on heavy-duty paper. I wanted to glue the portrait in a folder as a protected, permanent thing. So I generously applied glue to the back of the folder instead of the back of the picture. I placed the picture inside, closed the folder, and put Mother's heavy unabridged dictionary, eight inches thick, on top of it. When I came back the next day, I took the dictionary and folder off and the entire finish of the table came off: an 11 x 14 patch of bare wood. Actually, Mom thought it was kind of humorous, and I didn't get in trouble. She encouraged my creativity in photography, and this encouragement transcended almost everything I did when I got into trouble in the house. Mom saw the humor in most of my antics, and never blamed me, even for the fire, which I accidentally started when I was ten. And this stood me in good stead for forty years, when I fixed on the creativity I had. I had been sort of unbridled as a kid.

* * *

I took hundreds of pictures of family and friends. I always made copies and went down to the basement after dinner to develop them. Sometimes on the weekend I would stay there almost all night long, until the wee hours of the morning. I made pictures of Aunt Lucy and Uncle Maury and the grandparents. Dad always wanted copies. There was an incident that showed the yin and the yang about Mom. When I was at Whitefish Bay High, my freshman or sophomore year, I got the opportunity to be the photographer of the school paper, the *Tower Times*. Another boy wanted to be the yearbook photographer and had all the fancy equipment. I only had a Leica that Dad gave me. I went to the photography store in Whitefish Bay. I knew I wanted a Roloflex, a very expensive German camera. While I was looking at the stuff in the store this guy walked in with two Roloflexes. He needed to sell them for an operation on his foot. He wanted a hundred bucks for each camera. I said, "I'll give you $125 for each one, but I have to check them out." You know how trusting people are. Or were back then. He let me take them out of the store to another photography shop. They checked out perfectly and I bought them.

I got the job of photographer for the *Tower Times*. Mother asked me, "Why isn't your name on the masthead?" Mom was ticked off and nagged me incessantly to get my name on. She was doing it for me. But it was also a big, internal, projected need of her own to be recognized. And I discovered one of the greatest tragedies of her life. She felt she never got the professional recognition she deserved. No matter how much she received, she badly needed more. She pressured me and pressured me. Well, I went to the prom and took 300 pictures. That was thirty rolls of film, and I made proofs and they wanted them for the Whitefish Bay High yearbook. You might say I blackmailed the teacher, who was the adviser to the yearbook and *Tower Times*. I said, "I won't give you the prom photos until I get my name on the masthead of the paper and credit in the yearbook." They were going to press, so she agreed. This was the beginning. I took pictures at the school plays and made 8 x 10s and placed them on the bulletin board after the plays were over. The school paid me and I made a lot of money. They cost me ten cents apiece.

* * *

All these letters I used to get at camp—they came on colored stationery from Mother. She had the most incredible handwriting, florid, beautiful. The letters were amusing and fun to get. The interesting thing about this—Dad never wrote letters. After Mom died I was really angry that he wouldn't write me. I was home from college for the summer. I was so angry I was actually going to leave home. I was packing! I told Dad why I was so angry and he said writing letters was awkward for him. He'd tried dictating and that didn't work. But he did start writing letters to me, and that was the beginning of forty years of letters between us.

The strangest thing happened to me the other day. I was having coffee with Ann and told her I don't remember Mother ever reading books. I don't remember seeing her quietly sitting in a room reading books. Rosemary, perhaps you remember I was never that good a reader. Your ex-husband recommended books to me, but all my adult life I never read more than five books a year. Then I bought a Kindle. Now I read sixty-five books a year.

That memory of Mother's lack of reading books . . . She was always doing research—for her articles and her own book, of course. What I remember is her writing, writing, writing—the typewriter clacking, clacking, and the next morning balls of paper on the floor of the den.

* * *

One of my favorite memories is the poodle skirts Mom and her club were making for charity. Sitting on the floor with all that felt, rubbing your hands all over it, silhouettes of the poodles, moving them around. Pink felt with black poodles. I was just fascinated by this stuff, all this business with the poodles and Christmas wrappings and the colorful costumes Mother used to make for us. It all sparked an interest in me in fashion, which I still have to this very day. She was willing to try anything. She encouraged me to try new things, but I didn't have a lot of patience. So she bought me a clock, an owl: a pendulum plastic clock that you hung on a wall. It needed to be assembled. It came with graphite to lubricate the plastic gears. I had on a white shirt. The clock got a good dose of graphite on it and so did my white shirt. Mom didn't mind. That was perfectly all right in her book. That was a very very good part of my memories of her encouraging my creativity.

* * *

One of my more serious memories of Mom comes with mixed feelings. She demanded that we care for family. Every Sunday we couldn't plan a thing, even in high school. Sunday was for visiting the four grandparents. Of course, there was always Passover and Thanksgiving with the whole family and grandparents. Dad's brother Maury Pollack and Josephine were coming from California. I made a crack and groaned, "They're a bore." And did Mom get on my case! "They're family and you take care of them." I am blessed by being taken care of by so many family members. That odd complex duality of Mother pressuring and demanding and doing something she had such strong feelings for. Now, in retrospect, I think it may have been her unconscious need to be treated with respect by other members of the family. It was hard for her. She often felt alone. Her high intellect made it hard for her to relate to other people, because they weren't often on her level.

* * *

She took delight in her own jokes. To this day, when I tell jokes I love laughing at them myself. I really don't care how other people feel about it, I feel it's funny and laugh about it. This was contagious. Mom saw humor in many, many things, and it's amazing she was able to keep this humor until the end of her life, even with her anemia and other health problems, and the duality of her needs, pressuring others to do what she wanted. She really was a woman with enormous contrasts. She had such high energy and creativity and sometimes neurotic, demanding behavior. There wasn't much middle ground with Mom. I remember Rosemary in a table-setting contest and Mother forcing her ideas on her.

I was running around with my friend Dick Sweet. Dick's girlfriend had her cousin visiting, a very nice young kid and she had an incredibly large nose. Mom was in our gazebo in the backyard. We're all sitting there chatting. Then we were going to leave and Mom said to Dick's cousin, "It was so nose of you to come." We all cracked up, including the girl. A very long-lasting fun memory.

* * *

I always struggled in school tremendously. My emotional immaturity, pressures from Mom to succeed; not so much from Dad, he was busy being a doctor. But Mom never ever stopped telling me I was smart, reinforcing the idea that knowledge is power and that everything is available in the world, and all you have to do is look for it. She did a lot of research for her writing. I have an absolutely incurable curiosity, and that's a good thing. I can't walk by anything without wanting to learn about it. Walking through a room, touching something, or in a store, I have to find out what it is, how it works. Friends say they don't remember a single subject that I don't know something about. There's also this business that I wanted to be independent. This thing started in my head. If you want something, you can do something to get it. You've just got to go do it. You can't just sit back and wait for it. That stuck with me with a tenacity and allowed me to overcome colitis and other disadvantages, and to do my story telling and achieve business success.

* * *

The common bond in the family was the dog, Blaze. He meant everything to me and affected my life and my feelings about dogs today. My thousands of dreams and fantasies have involved dogs. When Mother died he moped around and hung around the bedroom for a long time. I remember the kitchen table, his head in my lap, and I'd feed him and Mom watched his tail wagging at the other end of the table and reminded me, "Don't feed the dog."

* * *

There's a really important lesson that Mom taught me. I sat behind a guy named Jim Porter in high school, just at the beginning of high school. I didn't have many friends at that time. He was an awfully smart guy and very creative. He would draw cartoons, like ones that made fun of teachers. He liked cars. His father was a lawyer and owned a sports car, a Jaguar. He also had a Mercedes 300SL, one of the most classic sports cars of all time; a gull-wing sports car; and a white Lincoln convertible.

I came home one day and said I didn't have many friends. Mom said, "Who do you want to be friends with?"

"This guy named Jim Porter," I told her. "He's real smart and I'm not smart."

Here's what Mom told me. "You're smart. You show an interest in what he's doing. Start with that and see what happens." She laid out a road map on how to become his friend. I started reading car magazines, collecting them, and showed him one. He was interested in photography too. I showed him my camera, the Roloflex. Any time I want to make friends I go back to that original lesson. Do it slowly and never tell what you're doing. Jim had a friend, Denise, who was an artist. I paid her $25 and she made a pastel portrait of Blaze, a wonderful likeness. I gave it to you, Rosemary, and we gave it to Dad. I still have it after all those years. Without my friendship with Jim, I wouldn't have that portrait.

And I can tell you this without reservation. I don't want a relationship with everybody, but if I want a relationship with somebody, they don't stand a chance. I'll have a relationship. That was all from what Mom taught me, from her guidance and training.

My friend Dick Sweet was going to Wisconsin, a straight-A student. I'm a C student and I'm going, too. He agreed to be my roommate freshman year. Then I find out he's picked Jim Rosenbaum to be his roommate. I was absolutely devastated. I went home and cried and cried. This was being such a traitor to our friendship. I was beside myself. Mom counseled me. She said, "This incident cannot destroy a whole friendship or shouldn't, and don't let it." She convinced me to forgive him. I went my freshman year and I got a sophomore as a roommate. He was a crazy sonofabitch from Chicago, really a character, and I enjoyed him.

I remained friends with Dick and never roomed with him, even though we were in the same fraternity. We socialized our entire college career and went our separate ways after. That experience reminded me of Mom's advice on how to handle a friendship that at first had disappointed me. She made me understand the value of keeping your head on straight and not taking things too personally. That was really the lesson I learned, mostly from a lot of psychoanalysis. I was able to develop friendships and forgive people. I remained a really strong straight rudder all these years from that input.

Now that I'm thinking about it, I'm sure Mother didn't forgive a lot of people in her life. She cared so much about us, but she didn't have such great control over her own emotional turmoil, and that was the enigma.

* * *

I was sixteen and had just gotten my driver's license. During my first week driving, I was caught by the Whitefish Bay Police. Our village police force amounted to one guy, who had his office in the basement of the Whitefish Bay Library. It was my first ticket from this policeman. I was going thirty miles an hour in this twenty miles per hour school zone. In those days the police handled things on a very casual basis compared to today. He notified my parents. Dad went with me to the Police Department. He was upset; propriety was very important to him. Dad took the car keys away for a week. That was a really big thing, getting stopped by the police.

Love! Laugh! Panic!

That night at dinner, Mom brought dessert to the table and she set down this huge chocolate cake—totally black, the whole damned thing had black frosting on it. Plus a card with a black border: "To our son in his greatest hour of need." Dad was furious as hell that she treated it with such humor, and I responded by eating most of the cake myself. Mom didn't stop there. She knew people on the staff of the *Milwaukee Journal*, which ran a Sunday column of local happenings called "All Things Considered." The following Sunday an item began: "A prominent Milwaukee psychiatrist . . ." It detailed the story about my ticket and the cake. Dad was even more livid, but he couldn't do anything about it. Many years later he laughed, too.

He got his revenge when Mom turned forty. She was really upset. "At forty you're not a young woman anymore. I don't want any kind of party, just something quiet."

"Fine," Dad said. "I agree." He secretly set up a large surprise party, and to top it all off, he got a can of whitewash and painted "40" on each window in the house facing the street. Next, he made a foot-high banner saying "40th Birthday" to go over the front door. Finally, he took our large wicker laundry basket and filled it with presents.

Mother was stunned, blushed furiously, and then began to laugh. She knew she'd been had. She got over it, of course, when she received Dad's special gift, an 18-karat-gold charm bracelet. The charms included a replica of Mother's book cover with the title engraved on it; Dad's medical school fraternity pin; a trolley car; a mandolin; a golf bag containing a putter; a mini-cameo; and a cocktail shaker—when you opened the top a tiny devil popped up.

It wasn't until after the guests had left that Dad took her outside to show her the windows and banner.

Chapter 9

On Being a Bad Sister—Sometimes

I have this totally unproductive, wasteful habit of shoulda, woulda, coulda. I rake over my life's coals. *I should have done better, or something different.* Even today. One of these most intense moments is feeling that I didn't protect John the way I could have. But I was, in some ways, terrified of my parents, especially Mother.

It was a dictatorial era. When I was fourteen, I could not defy Mother. I grew up not thinking for myself very well or very often. John, at age eleven, came home from school one afternoon, tossed his books on the couch, and began playing with Blaze. Mother burst into an irrational scold, shouting: "Stop rolling around on the floor with the dog! Go outside and play!" John went outside. What I wanted to interject and was just too tongue-tied to say was: "John has had a hard day at school and he's home now and it's his time to relax. Why can't he roll around on the floor with Blaze? It's his dog. You bought it for him."

So here I am today still reminded of that unpleasant moment and still wishing I had come to his rescue.

My sister-in-law Ann, on reading the manuscript of this book, said I have too much guilt. "You were young, you didn't know," she said. She's right. Recently, psychologist John Rosemond wrote in his newspaper column "Parent Power": "Above all else, keep the demons of guilt at bay. Guilt is the enemy."

In many ways, my brother is very much like Father. He has a deeply accurate perception of people, a fantastic sense of humor, and tremendous creativity. As a mechanical engineer in heavy-equipment sales, he used his understanding of people profitably. He was hosting a group of Texas businessmen, and in the car, he popped in a cassette of country music. The men all started singing. John knew how to tune into people, which gave him an edge in his profession.

Yes, he loves his own jokes, all jokes and comic situations. He has a bellowing laugh that used to drive Father to exasperation, hunching over with his hands covering his face. When Father took us to see *Fiddler on the Roof* on Broadway, John's bellowing bass overrode the entire audience's laughter. Even today, in a restaurant, the walls vibrate. He says so many funny things, just his take on life, that I laugh too. Ann rolls her eyes and says, "Don't encourage him."

I also recall times when I did an okay job of sistering. I took him to the movies—at the Shorewood Theater, twelve cents a ticket—to see *Lassie Come Home*. Sensitive little John was so affected by Lassie in trouble, that I had to take him out to the lobby for a few minutes.

When he was nine, Mother let me take him to the movie *The Secret Life of Walter Mitty*, starring Danny Kaye. It's based on a short story by James Thurber about a milquetoast husband who lives in a fantasy world, where he is a person of great power in every profession. Late that night, I was in bed and heard a noise. My room was at the top of the stairs. I quietly opened my door and peeked out. A lamp was on in the living room. There sat my brother, on the couch, wearing Father's fedora and Mother's white gloves. On the coffee-table were a deck of cards and a jigger of Coke with the bottle next to it. One of Mother's cigarettes (unlit, of course) drooped from the side of his mouth. With gloved hands he fanned his cards. John was Walter Mitty, famed riverboat gambler.

* * *

While I was at Camp Pinemere, John went much farther north to Camp Horseshoe in Hayward, Wisconsin, near Lake Superior. He wrote the required postcards home, always signing them "John Roger Pollack" to remind us who he was. And for a week after he returned, he sat at the dinner table hunched over, with his left arm curved around his plate to protect it from other boys filching his food.

John had a friend, "Eddie," across the street. Whenever the

two played together, somehow trouble happened. Father and his friends had made me a recreation room for my thirteenth birthday. Down on their knees, late into the night, fueled by scotch, they created a linoleum tile floor. The gooey mastic stunk and was terrifically hard to work with. But the floor turned out great. Shortly after my party, John and Eddie were playing down there and they decided to explore the function of a small fire-extinguisher can. Huge white blotches dotted the new floor. Forever.

There was something about Eddie and his family. At his house, when he and John were horsing around in their basement, John saw an open door and wondered what was in it. Eddie slammed it shut. "We're not allowed in there," he said.

One afternoon I came home from school to find Mother standing at the window, chuckling, arms across her chest as she gazed across the street. Police cars were lined up in front of Eddie's house. Officers emerged from inside, carrying telephones and other stuff. The next day the papers carried the story. The secret room was used by Eddie's father to run a numbers racket. They moved shortly after.

Wall-to-wall carpeting was installed in our house, a rich pearl-gray; the same carpeting that our darling Blaze so rudely disrespected weeks later. Only a few hours after installation, Mother went into the living room to admire and inspect. From upstairs we heard a prolonged shriek. "John!" The whole house trembled in fear. We rushed down to find her standing over a large blob of black ink. She bent down to touch it. Lo and behold, the blob was plastic. Clever John. Nevertheless, she had trouble laughing at this prank. Another side of her relationship to her son: If he had been living in Tokyo at that moment, she would still have yelled "John!"

What's fascinating is that, to this day, many of his memories coincide with my own. John recalled the poodle skirts. Mother was vice president of the College Women's Club in the early Fifties. She dreamed up their successful fundraiser for college scholarships: making circle skirts that were all the rage and selling them. I even joined the ladies on their knees in our living room, cutting out huge rounds of felt, on which they appliquéd horses or butterflies or poodles. And then jeweled them. No ordinary bake sales for

Love! Laugh! Panic!

Mother.

Mother's craft skills didn't get into my DNA. She once made me a lovely Queen Esther costume for our Purim parade at temple. When my Miriam was in Sunday School, I indulged in an impulse purchase of pink organdy material with white flocking, a large remnant on sale. I intended to make my daughter a Queen Esther gown. Spreading the fabric out on the dining room table, I suddenly woke up, so to speak, and said aloud, "Wait a minute. I don't know how to make a dress!" I stuck the fabric in a drawer and gave it to our artist daughter Myrna—forty years later.

Then there was my adventure in knitting. At Smith, in my Art 11 survey course, each lecture consisted of dozens of slides of famous artworks and architecture. I took notes nonstop; there was so much to learn. But some of the girls didn't. They were busy knitting. Knitting? Argyle socks, no less. I was spellbound. The bobbins hung down, swinging with the motion of the needles. How could those knitters be paying attention? Did they have photographic memories? Nevertheless, I decided there must be something to this business, so I bought myself the makings of argyle socks for Father. The colors I chose were light blue, fuchsia, black, and white. Never mind that argyles are not exactly for beginners. Never mind that Father didn't wear bright plaids of anything. Over the next few months I managed to knit the socks (but not in class) down to the ankles. But I had no idea how to make the feet. And by then I was bored silly. I took them home, not even thinking to ask Aunt Lucy for her expertise, and stuck them in a drawer in the guest room. Three decades later, after Father died at age eighty-six, I discovered them in the drawer—and threw them away.

I can't believe I did that. Today I'm a rabid recycler. I'd at least send the half-socks and paraphernalia to a charity. When our girls came to visit in Severna Park, I got on their case if they threw away Styrofoam takeout containers. We recycled everything in Anne Arundel County. Styrofoam stays in the landfill for forty to sixty years. Now I'll get off my soapbox. But not for long, as Larry knows.

I'm amazed that John remembers my disastrous table-setting adventure, because it didn't involve him. It was a girls' thing. But it was also a perfect example of how sometimes Mother got obnoxiously pushy in her drive to help us succeed.

In high school I was a member of the Girls' Club. Junior year our teacher/adviser arranged for us to enter a table-setting contest. We would be competing just against each other in teams of two. Gimbel's department store sponsored the contest, quite a clever promotion for them, actually. Our settings were to be displayed in their gift department. The store allowed each team to choose a silver pattern that would dictate the theme of our table. Then we were on our own to create any kind of table décor we wanted. The gift department managers would do the judging. My partner, Marcia, and I chose a seashell pattern.

That's when Mother threw herself into our project. She didn't ask us what we thought of her ideas or if we wanted her help. She brought our the Royal Worcester china with its rich blue rim and our dessert dishes of wavy green, nobby glass. Blue-green ocean waves, I guess she had in mind. Then she came up with a brainstorm for the centerpiece: a large goldfish bowl filled with live goldfish. Marcia and I were so bowled over (pun intended) that we didn't protest or even suggest that we be left alone to invent our own setting. Bottom line: We were one of six teams—and we came in last place! The killer was the fishbowl. The judges said a centerpiece of live fish was unappetizing.

When we returned home and reported the bad news to Father, he just shook his head and said, "I knew that would happen."

Larry and I have taken many lovely sightseeing trips with John and Ann. The British Isles; Portugal and Spain; Thailand and Cambodia; New Zealand and Australia; Japan; Egypt; and in the U.S.

On a visit to them in Minnesota, we explored Red Wing, Taylor's Falls, and the Potholes in Interstate State Park. These gaping holes, deep and filled with icy water, were carved eons ago from glacial runoff. John's love of Blaze led him to a heroic moment there, but one he's much too modest to ever talk about. It was mid-October, plenty nippy in the late afternoon. A flock of tourists clustered around the wrought-iron security fence, including one family standing next to us with their golden retriever. Suddenly, the dog got loose and squeezed between the bars. Maybe it was trying to get to the water to drink. It slipped and fell into the pothole, shivering, the frigid water up to its neck. The family just stood there, baffled. Without even considering his personal safety, John climbed over the fence. Reaching down, he cupped his arms under the frightened, trembling dog and lifted it out, returning it to the family. John's jacket was muddy and soaked. They didn't even say thank you.

It's in the genes, the creativity. John has spent many years volunteering as a master storyteller in the schools—even during his successful engineering career. He's a real spellbinder, my brother.

* * *

What I'm realizing now is that—by the time John reached high school—he was closer to Mother than I was. He felt freer to tell her his problems; his openness allowed her to help him come up with solutions. When I was a thousand miles away, my senior year at Smith, it was John who drove her to her chemotherapy appointments.

* * *

On my graduation day, I received this telegram:

"Rosie. You know that I am always proud of my sister. But tonight I am especially proud. You have worked hard and bucked a lot to be able to graduate from Smith. In fact, I wouldn't even trade you in for a new camera. All my love, John."

Chapter 10

Aunt Lucy

My Aunt Lucy had quite a stellar history of her own. In Milwaukee her Sunday School teacher was Golda Meir, future prime minister of Israel.

Harry Bragarnick insisted that all four of his children get a college education. Mother and Dorothy graduated from the University of Wisconsin: mother in journalism, Dorothy in education. Dorothy taught Honors English in Washington, D.C.; one of her students, Ann Beattie, became a well-known novelist. Robert attended the Wharton School of Business at the University of Pennsylvania. Late in his career, he designed *Food and Wine,* a magazine still flourishing today.

Lucy, in those days, was able to go straight from high school to Marquette University Law School. The State Bar of Wisconsin published a booklet in 1998, *Pioneers in the Law: The First 150 Women.* The section about Lucile Bragarnick includes this anecdote:

"Several weeks before graduation from Marquette University Law School, she learned that she was short a geometry credit from high school and was not qualified to graduate. In consulting her advisor, he said if she was not a good enough lawyer to defend her own case, she didn't deserve to graduate. Her defense was that, although her failure to finish geometry was clearly her fault, the university should never have let her get that far without it. The university agreed, and she received her degree."

Lucy was the first woman in the state of Wisconsin to graduate from law school. She passed the bar exam, but in 1930, the heart of the Great Depression, jobs for women attorneys "were not readily available."

Love! Laugh! Panic!

She had just married Maurice Ostrow. To help him through dental school, she went to work in her parents' hosiery and dry goods store—not exactly a glamorous locale for a young professional woman. Situated in an old, rather run-down neighborhood on North Twelfth Street, the store had creaking linoleum floors and fluorescent fixtures that cast a sallow light.

Speaking of the store, Robert, as a Wharton graduate in 1938, gave his father some golden advice. "Nylon stockings. They're the future." That advice helped create Harry's fortune.

Lucy and Mother loved each other dearly, but the sisters had emotional tussles that somehow never got resolved. Lucy was only fourteen months older, but early on, Grandma and Grandpa placed her in a quite adult role. When Mother was in high school, she would breeze into the family store and announce that she was going to a football game. Grandma and Grandpa never chastised her or demanded that she too help out. Of course Lucy resented her for it.

Lucy let her hair grow white. Mother always colored hers her normal light brown. Lucy was attractive, but needlessly looked twenty years older than she was. On their side of the family women grayed early. I inherited this unfortunate tradition. At twenty-nine I was going gray. Bummer! So I followed Mother's path and color my hair to this day.

Aunt Lucy and Uncle Maury lived four blocks from us. I loved going over there. When my cousin Susan was at camp, Aunt Lucy allowed me to lie on Susan's twin bed for hours, reading her enormous collection of love comics. At home I had a comic book of Bible stories. My favorite was Adam and Eve on the pages where they wore those fig leaves.

Mostly, I collected movie magazines. I had crushes on Ronald Reagan as a rancher fighting anthrax. Van Johnson, so clean-cut. Marlon Brando—oh my God, so hot. Mom and Dad saw *A Streetcar Named Desire* on Broadway. Even Mother said he exuded animal magnetism.

The sisters talked on the phone every day. Often they would get into some argument, Mother the liberal, Lucy the conservative, utterly traditional. After ten minutes they'd hang up on each other. A few hours later, Mother would be back on the phone asking Lucy for her veal chops recipe, which she simply couldn't remember. It got to be a family joke. Too embarrassed to call yet again, she had me call. Lucy always laughed and good-naturedly gave it to me. Eventually, it got written down.

Here it is, loosely remembered, Aunt Lucy's Famous Veal Chops recipe. Pre-heat the oven to 350°. Start with a large box of cornflakes. Use a rolling pin to crush them fine. Dredge (dip) the chops in milk, shake off the excess, and roll them in the cornflake crumbs. Spray cooking oil on a 9 x 12 Pyrex dish and place the chops in it. Bake at 350° for 45 minutes.

Aunt Lucy was an accomplished and creative cook. On Sundays we were allowed a treat: her homemade apricot jam laced with blanched-almond slivers and bits of maraschino cherries.

She was Mrs. Neaty-Neat incarnate. When John and I spent the night, we discovered her ritual of carpet-sweeping the living room at 10 p.m. No going to bed without it. The joke was that if we went to the bathroom in the middle of the night, we'd find our beds made when we came back.

Uncle Maury died at sixty-five of cancer. His last months were horrific. He was angry, lashing out at his fate and the frustration of no cure on the horizon. Lucy begged him to stop raging so that the last phase of their life together could be more pleasant and bearable. Uncle Maury had been such a wonderful, accommodating husband. He was a pharmacist when they married, but Lucy urged him to become a dentist. Which he did. As his patient when I was growing up, even as a child I got the feeling he wasn't very happy being a dentist.

In her early eighties, Lucy still lived in her own apartment in the Shorewood suburb of Milwaukee, even though she had Parkinson's disease. One evening John, Ann, and I arrived for a visit and saw an ambulance parked at the curb. We felt a moment of panic. Was it for Lucy?

Yes. Friends had invited her out to dinner and brought her home. Lucy wanted to get ready for bed, but couldn't undo the buttons on the back of her blouse. So she called 911! The young female EMT, courteous and respectful, had a slight smile on her face. We got the impression this wasn't the first time she'd been

Love! Laugh! Panic!

summoned to undo buttons.

Chapter 11

Together in the Kitchen —for Better or Worse

"This is what we have for dinner and this is what you will eat. Perhaps tomorrow night we will have what you like."

That was Mother's mantra when John or I sat down to the table to some dish we couldn't stand. For John, it was vegetable soup. For me, sweetbreads and beet borscht. Mother served the Russian soup cold with a dollop of sour cream—and that was the only good thing about it. Swirling it round and round until the reddish-purple soup turned pink. And then not eating it.

In 1948 I started helping Mother cook. I was eight. Dinner was a major production, of course—labor-intensive, at least an hour. Not like today. No frozen foods, nothing prepackaged, no microwave. Still, I loved helping. Her bible was *The Settlement Cookbook*, with its blue oilcloth cover. I still have it. She taught me everything she'd ever learned. Some of it I actually digested, figuratively speaking. We got along better when we cooked than at any other time. A few of my special assignments:

- A tall grocery bag of loose spinach. "Take off the stems and make sure each leaf is fresh, not black and shriveled." It always struck me as a big deal, considering the end result, when the cooked spinach, vastly shrunk, sat meekly in its bowl.
- Iceberg lettuce for salad: "Tear the leaves, don't cut them." Did the leaves feel less pain that way?
- Artichokes, a rare treat: "Take the scissors and snip off the tips off the largest leaves horizontally."

- Asparagus. "Cut off the tough bottoms. Take a paring knife and pull off the little triangles on each stalk."
- To clean fresh mushrooms: "Swirl them around in a bowl of warm, salty water."
- Baking a cake from scratch: Alternate the dry and wet ingredients. "Start with flour, end with flour."

I learned to use our Foley Food Mill to grind up leftover pot roast for hash. I liked fitting the sturdy steel appliance to the edge of the kitchen table and turning the large key-screw to secure it. And cranking the handle over and over, watching the pulverized food plop into the waiting bowl. The night before one Thanksgiving, with company coming, my parents went out. Mother had cooked the cranberries for sauce. I used the food mill to puree them. So proud of my initiative—unappreciated, it turned out. "I had planned to serve the cranberries whole."

A chicken from the Kosher butcher came with skin that was fairly smooth, but not entirely plucked. Mother would sear it on a hot plate set on the gas stove, then use tweezers to yank out the last of the pinfeathers.

When they were first married, Mother planned to serve Father fish, but worried that he might not like even the sound of "fish."

"What's for dinner?" he asked.

"Shellfonti," Mother said, a name she'd made up ten minutes before. He liked it.

Mother sympathized with Father's sixty-hour-a-week medical practice and how important dinner was. Sometimes she'd make one of his favorite dishes: baked eggplant. She took a large whole eggplant and set it on the hot plate on the stove, searing it slowly until the skin was charred, then turned it to a fresh spot until the entire eggplant was black. Inside it was soft, completely cooked. Mother sliced off the top as if it were a soft-boiled egg and set it vertically on Father's plate. He ate the whole thing with a fork.

I baked my first cake from scratch (there was no other way) that year, for Uncle Maury's birthday. After sliding the single layer onto the oven rack, I ran outside to play. What a shock when I pulled the cake tin out of the oven. Instead of a masterpiece with a smooth surface, I was staring at a crater the size of Mount Etna.

"Mom!" I wailed.

"You let the screen door slam when you went outside and the loud bang made the cake fall."

"Don't worry, Mom," I said. "I'll just fill the center up with frosting." She suppressed a smile and allowed me to mix up a whole batch to find out for myself that you can't feed guests an inch of cake and three inches of butter-cream frosting. Ruefully, I dumped the cake in the garbage and started over.

We had pigeons in our backyard and one laid an egg. So exciting! Sunday morning, little John woke our parents early to report: "I ate the pigeon egg for my breakfast."

We had no air conditioning. Who did in the Fifties? In our suburb a mile from Lake Michigan, the summers were hot and humid. You could fold the Saltines in half. Wanting to be thrifty and not waste them, Mother routinely put them under the broiler to crisp them up. Then she'd disappear into the den for a quick phone call. Five minutes later, smoke poured out of the broiler—crackers burnt black. Into the garbage.

Another victim of our weather was Fluffy White Frosting. Mother taught me to make it—with an egg white, cream of tartar, sugar, vanilla, and boiling water, all beaten together until the frosting stood in peaks. But I learned the hard way not to make it on a humid day. The fluffy frosting quickly developed air holes. Not a pretty sight and not servable.

She attended a Cordon Bleu cooking class, a lecture course for experienced cooks. John and I never got to eat the beef Stroganoff made with flat champagne or the chocolate roll. They were strictly for company. The chocolate roll turned into a crisis every time. As she was rolling up the thick layer of cream-filled cake, it always cracked.

Mother sometimes went a little nuts trying to get us to toe the line. John didn't want to finish his leftover vegetable soup at lunch. Mother made it either too watery or too thick—or something. So he added salt. That didn't help. Then sugar. Now it tasted even worse. "You can't leave the table until you finish it!" Twelve-thirty. One o'clock. Finally, Mother got fed up (pun intended). As soon as she left the kitchen and I heard her footsteps reaching the second floor, I took the bowl and dumped the soup into the powder-room toilet. I called upstairs: "Mom, he finished it!"

Deli-style tongue, sliced and roasted with onions and gravy. But first Mother boiled the tongue. Creepy—this giant thing swaying this way and that against the waves of bubbling water. It reminds me of the one time my ex-husband and I steamed live crabs that we'd bought at the City Dock in Annapolis. We could hear the crabs clawing against the sides of the tall pot as they tried to get out. Never again.

After school John and I sometimes toasted marshmallows, spearing them onto forks over the gas stove. We didn't pay much attention and allowed the melted, gooey stuff to land on the burners, clinging, hardening; a mess for ticked-off Mother to clean.

My parents especially liked Farmer's Chop Suey. Chopped fresh tomatoes, cucumbers, radish slices, and scallions, mixed together in sour cream. After moving to the East Coast I never saw it again. When I told Larry about this concoction, he gave me a quizzical look. "I've never heard of it. I bet your mother made it up." Ha! I Googled it. Farmer's Chop Suey is alive and well and sometimes known as Jewish Chop Suey.

Some of Mother's light desserts just magically appeared on the table, but I have no idea how she made them: Prune Whip, Floating Island, and Pink Junket. On Sunday nights our family took Grandma Minnie and Grandpa Henry to Ming Gardens, a Chinese restaurant. The dessert I remember best is kumquats. They looked like tiny oval oranges, stewed in their thick juice. I've never since seen kumquats on the menu in any restaurant, Chinese or otherwise.

Venetian Torte was the *pièce de résistance* for Mother, Lucy—and me! (That is, until I discovered supermarket bakeries thirty years ago.)

A Venetian Torte is made up of six layers: three sponge cake layers sliced horizontally, filled and totally covered with chocolate whipped cream. The first time Mother baked it she left the three layers to cool on the counter. Returning an hour later to make the frosting, she found only two. Blaze was standing on his hind legs, gobbling up the last bite of the third layer.

Fresh out of college, living in Boston with my roommate, we gave our first dinner party in our ninety-dollar-a-month apartment on Myrtle Street, on Beacon Hill. For dessert I made my Venetian Torte. Too skillfully, it turned out. It stood so high that each slice needed a dinner plate. Our guests, already full from our big meal, stared in dismay.

Our house on Woodburn Street was three blocks from school. We came home for lunch. When Mother had to be out at lunchtime, she left lovely sandwiches in the fridge with a note for each of us.

* * *

Eventually, I learned what *not* to serve company; besides foot-high slices of Venetian Torte. My ex and I served a dinner of barbecued spare ribs, sauerkraut, and potato salad. Fine, but for dessert, how about lemon sorbet? Not Baked Alaska. It was too heavy. And so much work! For a dinner in our Manhattan apartment, a third-floor walkup with no air conditioning, what did I serve on a 90-degree day? An Indian curry stew, piping hot, on rice.

When Larry and I were newlyweds, we served a lovely brisket at our first dinner party. Two friends surprised us by confessing they didn't eat beef, so they were stuck with our salad, potatoes, and whatever. In the salad I had included thin slices of fresh zucchini. One of these friends didn't like that either. She's a highly organized person. When I cleared her plate away, I discovered two neat stacks of zucchini slices—one green stack, one yellow.

I gave solo dinner parties during my divorced years. One was to be a special treat for my loving Aunt Dorothy and Uncle Poke. As I set the shrimp casserole on the table, Aunt Dorothy announced that she was allergic to shellfish. But she'd neglected to tell me this in advance. Then she described what happened to her on a flight from Hong Kong to New York. Dinner included salad with shrimp scattered on top. Uncle Poke removed them, but there must have been shrimp juice left on the lettuce. She got instantly sick and bolted for the lavatory. Inside, she vomited so profusely that she sank to the floor, leaning against the door. She was in there so long the flight attendants were pounding on the door, trying to get in and help her (and, of course, because other passengers needed the lav). After listening to this gruesome story (before we sat down to the table, thankfully) I made her an omelet.

My friends who know I have Crohn's disease are probably snickering. "Rosemary should talk about letting a hostess know what she can't eat." The reason I don't inform a hostess is that my list of taboo foods goes from here to the moon. I've taken a new tack. "How about we meet at a restaurant?" Then we can happily socialize; the hostess doesn't have to concern herself with my list; and I don't have to reciprocate! So that's the best thing I've learned about giving dinner parties. Don't. And as far as cooking in general goes, I agree with author Shirley Conran (*Superwoman*, 1975), who said, "Life is too short to stuff a mushroom."

By the way, to learn more about my taboo foods, check out "Coping with Crohn's" on my personal blog. Go to our website, www.magicile.com. Click on "Rosemary's World." Now that I've mentioned my Crohn's, I should also mention that it's one of many stomach disorders prevalent among Eastern European Jews that can be inherited.

I think about Mother—her stomach problems and what she contended with day and night. Once on vacation in the Wisconsin Dells, she had a hankering for a chocolate ice cream sundae with chocolate sauce. In a drugstore we sat on the tall stools at the counter as Father ordered it. Mother took one spoonful and couldn't eat any more. Not that she didn't want to. Her gut rebelled and wouldn't allow her to.

Every day she had to take calcium. It came in powdered form and had to be mixed with half a glass of water. She had to drink it two or three times a day. The glass sat on the window ledge above the kitchen sink. It tasted horrid, "like chalk," she said. One afternoon Mother started drinking her calcium when she shouted in distress. The half-glass wasn't calcium. It was dish detergent that she had mixed with water to be thrifty, to use after the next meal. She had to call a poison-control center. They told her that, luckily, no lasting harm was done. *Oy vey!*

I think of what doing the laundry meant in those days, and how far we've come. Our wash machine had a ringer. I liked helping, but supervised by Mother. You had to feed the wet clothes through and make sure you didn't feed your hand and arm through, too. Then hang them up to dry outdoors with wooden clothespins. Then iron them. When Mother was a young bride, she was playing bridge with friends and bragged that she could iron one of Father's shirts in twelve minutes. The response was not what she expected. "You actually iron your husband's shirts?" The question was tinged with disdain. From that day on, his shirts went out to a laundry service.

Around 1950 Father bought Mother a dishwasher. This was a revolutionary appliance. It was a top loader, and the first time she used it, we all stuck around the kitchen to witness the wonderful finished product. Realizing the last cycle was complete, Mother hovered over it and eagerly waited. Up popped the top, clobbering her right under her chin.

Which reminds me. Larry and I were a little slow to get an updated refrigerator. In fact, we're still less than *avant garde*. Our new one, purchased in 2010, has a water dispenser—but inside. I bent over and stuck my head in a little way with my glass in hand, to see how the mechanism worked, and pushed the button. Next thing I knew, ice water was trickling down the back of my neck.

When the two men delivered that very same fridge, they didn't have a huge amount of space in which to maneuver it into the kitchen. The sharp top left edge of the fridge knocked against the globe of one of the two Tiffany-type fixtures over the dining room table. The large globe broke. Before the men left, one apologized for being careless and said he wanted to replace it. We told him it wasn't necessary. But he insisted.

"You know what I'm gonna do?" he said. "I'm gonna take this other globe with me so I can be sure to get the right size."

"No, no," I protested. "Please don't!" But it was too late. He had already unscrewed the perfectly good globe and tucked it under his arm.

"I'm gonna bring you two globes!" he said, triumphantly.

Guess what? We never heard from him again. Maybe he has a little business on the side, selling customers' globes.

Chapter 12

Grandma Minnie and Grandpa Henry

Whenever Grandma Minnie called and Mother answered the phone, her first words were always "How's Saul?" Never "How are *you*, Luby?" But Mother laughed about it. She was very good to her in-laws. When they came to our house they ate on paper plates because they kept Kosher. When my parents moved them closer to us from Milwaukee's far-away Brown Street, Mother did a lot of the moving and furniture arranging. She also bought them a beautiful painting of a rabbi for their living room.

Our Sunday ritual was to visit the four grandparents. Minnie and Henry Pollack and Elizabeth and Harry Bragarnick were best friends and lived only blocks apart. All four came to Milwaukee from Russia in the early 1900s to join family. At Ellis Island, when they were herded into an elevator, Minnie thought they were being weighed. She'd never been in an elevator before.

Mother and my father, four years older than she, grew up together. Saul was the youngest of five boys. In high school, Luby and Saul were good friends. For a Fourth of July bicycle parade, Luby dressed up as the Statue of Liberty. Saul helped her decorate her bike, with red, white, and blue streamers woven in and out of the wheel spokes. It was a grand, beautiful presentation until disaster struck. Luby fell off her bike and broke her arm.

Grandpa Henry worked for a store that sold light bulbs. He always asked for things during meals. "Minnie, the horseradish, Minnie, the salt." Minnie this or that. When Grandma had to get up to get it, then "Minnie, why aren't you sitting down?"

Love! Laugh! Panic!

When we were two or three years old, Grandpa Henry would put out one foot, let us climb on, and bounce us up and down, playing Horsey. Henry and Minnie were exceptionally kind, gentle, and loving.

Father brought Grandpa Henry to live with him after Grandma Minnie died. His memory was fading badly. He sat in our living room, dozing off with a cigarette between his fingers. Father feared a fire would start. A few months later, Grandpa stopped in my room and saw a pair of tall silver *Shabbat* candlesticks sitting on my shelf—the very same ones Father had polished every Friday from the time he was a little boy. Poor Grandpa, he stood there and cried. At that moment his memory was perfect, grieving for Grandma Minnie and their nearly seventy years together.

Chapter 13

Grandma Elizabeth and Grandpa Harry

Mr. and Mrs. Harry Bragarnick arrived at Ellis Island from Russia in 1913 with their two little girls, Luby, age five, and Lucy, seven. Mother's Russian name was Luba, meaning "beloved." The officials pressured Grandpa to change his complicated last name. He wouldn't hear of it. Harry had been a successful entrepreneur in Russia at the age of nineteen. He also had another job, as a "government rabbi." It had nothing to do with religion; he issued marriage licenses and such. Grandma taught elementary school. The family arrived at Ellis Island in handsome clothes, impressive enough to get excused from the required spraying for bugs. Grandpa had $68 in his pocket.

I was the first of seven grandchildren. When I was quite small, Grandpa pulled me to him at his desk and whispered in my ear: "If there's something you want that your parents won't give you, tell me. I'll give it to you." He gave me a ruby ring, which I wasn't responsible enough to own. I was fiddling with it on my finger in a restaurant. It fell off, and I didn't tell my mother about it for two days. She called the restaurant, and naturally, they couldn't find it. Grandpa didn't blame me; he gave me an amethyst ring to replace it.

Grandpa Harry had a commanding presence, even when he was just crossing the street. It didn't matter whether he was in a crosswalk or not. I saw him stroll into the middle of a street and hold up his cane, pointing it toward the oncoming cars. They always stopped for him.

Grandma Elizabeth's cooking and baking had unique qualities: elegance and an artistic flair of presentation. Her fruit platter at our Friday night *Shabbat* dinners had orange and grapefruit slices swirled around a platter like a gorgeous wheel. She taught Mother that you can serve hot dogs if you present them beautifully.

Once I watched Grandma make her strudel. The vast kitchen was twice the size of our family's living room. The kneaded dough was rolled out. You know how pizza bakers dramatically fling and twirl their dough for baking? Think rolled-out dough ten times the size of a large pizza and Grandma flinging it across the enormous table, ready to be cut into shapes. Grandpa Harry was an informal labor negotiator (see Chapter 14, "The Good Deed Man"). Grandma's strudel was a key element in the labor negotiations, held around the mahogany table in the Bragarnick apartment. Her strudel crust was exquisitely flaky, like phyllo dough, so the luscious crust and fruit melted in your mouth—and just about melted the tough stands of the negotiators.

At Christmastime, Grandma would also send her boxes of fresh strudel to our house for wrapping—to go to Grandpa's business associates and official contacts. Mother taught me the art of wrapping gifts, and wrapping these made me feel special and important. In the spare room, which she insisted on calling The Green Room, we sat for hours on the shag rug creating stunning packages. She taught me to make roses out of ribbons and how to create a more masculine package for men, with layered ribbon loops instead of a fluffy feminine look. How I loved those days.

For my college graduation, Grandpa and Grandma gave me a very grown-up ring: a blue star sapphire.

Chapter 14

The Good Deed Man, Part 1
By Luby Pollack

This article about Grandpa is reprinted from the *Wisconsin Jewish Chronicle*, May 7, 1948. "This is the first of two articles by Mrs. Pollack in which she gives a completely honest and objective report on her father, Harry Bragarnick, who will celebrate his 70th birthday this Sunday."

Last year a sobbing, shaking old man was robbed of his funeral suit, box, tissue paper and all right off a department store counter where he had just laid the cash.

Two days later the papers reported with glee that "The Good Deed Man Came Around Again," and told how Harry Bragarnick had read of the theft. He had bought a suit, some shirts, shoes and ties. He found a priest who found the man. And there it was. Once again the old fellow was "Ready to die" he said, "with respect."

It was just another good deed by Harry Bragarnick. Bragar-nick if you can pronounce it, just Mister B if you can't, is an excitable, nervous, imperious man. He has 70 years, thin, white hair, an elegant cane, and the most stubborn, chopped-up accent that ever afflicted an American speech.

We in Milwaukee have names for him other than the "Good Deed Man." He is Milwaukee's "Peacemaker," her "Impartial Arbitrator" and either "Altruist" or "Sucker" depending on which end of the glass you see to look at life.

Not that this bombastic Bragarnick ever just quietly "does" things. He seems to explode them with violence, zest and noise.

* * *

Love! Laugh! Panic!

Once our late Governor Walter Goodland watched Bragarnick leaving the capitol building at Madison. Goodland shook his head and smiled. "That man!" he said. "I have heard it said that if you live in Milwaukee one of two things can happen to you. Either you will go to Harry Bragarnick for a favor or he will come to you to force it on you." By now he was thoughtful and vigorously nodding his head. "Maybe so. He is one of the kindest human beings I ever knew." Any impression this incisive remark might give that Bragarnick stalks people to their very homes to do his good deeding is strictly intentional. If you have a problem and confide it to Bragarnick, he takes over, bing-bang. From then on your religious, your financial or your love life are yours no longer. They belong to Bragarnick and most of the time you give fervent thanks. Most of his good deeding is done from his home, a flat above his hosiery store, as paradoxical a place as its owner is a person. Outside, it is as shabby and run-down as the shabby business street on which it stands. Inside it is handsome, large, a well-furnished flat.

* * *

Often I have thought of that flat as a "house with a heart." Bragarnick has a big room that is his own, kind of a study. On the walls are testimonials from two governors, several mayors and Senator Barkley. It is kind of a court of human relations and people trek up the steps night and day.

There are rabbis and priests, ten-cent store clerks and very rich people. There are dull folks and Rhodes scholars, D.A.R.s and C.I.O.s. There was one ex-convict and several about-to-be convicts. There are judges and reporters and labor leaders and refugees. There are young people and old people and lots of just plain folks, Catholics, Protestants and Jews.

Once I was there when an anguished woman came stumbling up the stairs clutching her rosary and sobbing. Her garbage can was filled with dead people, she cried.

Bragarnick was gentle but he picked up the telephone and within a week the delusional sufferer was in a mental hospital receiving shock treatment.

Another time a man from Wyoming pounded up the stairs. He had just finished a stretch for forgery and he was carrying a bag. He was hostile and unpleasant and he snarled when he talked. "Understand," he told Bragarnick, "I didn't come to you for money, or for anything else. I read about you in a paper in Chicago and I came out of my way to find out what makes a damn fool like you click. What does it get you? I think you're a chump."

Two days later he had a job with a packing house. The letters he's still writing are on hotel stationery and on the top of the paper is his name as manager.

It isn't unusual for an Orthodox rabbi to come in the morning for a refreshing little talk on the Talmud, and in the afternoon for a gambler with a brand new yen for political office to come to tap the sounding board of Bragarnick's opinion. In one day a bank director came to ask him to sign affidavits to bring refugees to the States; an arthritic cripple came in a wheel chair for money for treatments; and two battling business partners screamed their injuries. At midnight of that very same day a desperate husband came begging for help. His wife was packing to leave him for good. His four young children, the eldest but eight, were all awake and crying at the strange behavior of their mom.

Bragarnick has a passion to give. It's such a big passion that it boils up, spills over and engulfs whomever is closest to his range of interest at that time.

Charity is a big item with him. If you ask him why he gives to charity so much out of proportion to his wealth he shrugs and says, "When it comes to giving I never consider to get poorer from giving. The more charity you give the more God gives you back." Another angle on the charity deal is that "Charity is taxes on life. Is that right or no? It's the same like taxes for your house or your business. You GOT to give. Charity you must give, is that right or no?"

Once years ago when he was quite poor, a Community Fund worker climbed the stairs to the flat above the hosiery store. Hesitantly she explained her mission. After a furtive glance around the modest furnishings, she asked could he, would he give $50. "No, I don't give $50" he said abruptly and strode from the room, while the lady fumbled an apologetic retreat. When she was almost out the door he yelled, "Wait a minute. You want I should give $200 or no?" He topped off the donation with a gallant gesture, a pair of silk stockings for the perspiring solicitor.

* * *

Parallel with this terrific urge to give is a shriveling contempt for the fellow who won't. "Him? That cheap pike?" His voice rises in indignation. "He's from the lowest of the low. He never gave a nickel, and when he did, what did he give? Penny-annie, that's is all. Penny-annie."

It would be an exquisite touch to say that this worthy who deliberately looks for people he can help, is tempered as the angels, soft, gentle and sweetly spoken. Nothing could be farther from the truth.

Harry Bragarnick, "Good Deed Man," is an extraordinary, cussed, ornery, difficult, generous, kind-hearted, arrogant, humble paradox. In Milwaukee he is thus known, appreciated and deprecated, both.

His vanity is of the super-colossal variety. It reflects not only in his custom-tailored suits, jeweled cuff links, narrow pointed calfskin shoes and, inevitably, a cane, sometimes with head of gold, sometimes of tortoise, but mostly of carved ivory in the shape of a bear's head, but in the way he talks about Bragarnick in a steady stream, given half a breath's chance.

He can stand dead-still in the middle of a room without moving or speaking, his white face suddenly cadaverous, and have his freezing blue eyes hurl enough bolts of lightning to frighten strong men. His temper is a touchy thing, flaring hot and quick; then he shouts and jerks about the room, the most outraged man in the universe, and if he still has a vestige of reasonableness left, it zips off like a kite in a typhoon. Then, heaven help the guy who's catching it.

* * *

He has told more people to go to hell, generally without just cause, than most dock wallopers, and absurdly enough, it is those he insults most flagrantly who come to him to apologize.

In twenty-odd years he hurled seven men down the steps of his upstairs flat. Today six of them are his good friends, the seventh is in jail for blackmail.

One of the six who got bounced was a prominent Milwaukee lawyer who came to propose that Bragarnick settle with a wholesale dry goods creditor [Landauer and Company]. The time was Depression; much of the stock in his small store was still on the shelves just as it was in other "penny-annie" dry goods stores. Most of the others were folding up like dropped fans. Bragarnick just wouldn't.

As soon as he had tossed the lawyer down the steps he grabbed his hat and stormed down to the wholesale house of Landauer and Company. In the credit manager's office he furiously demanded to know how he dared show him, Bragarnick, such an affront. The credit manager was grave. Business was bad everywhere, he said. It was no slur on Bragarnick. To make it easier for Bragarnick, the company was willing to make a 40 cent on the dollar settlement.

Bragarnick's face was ashen, almost as white as his hair. He strode to the desk. With clenched fist he pounded and shouted, "For me there is no settlements. When I owe, I pay, not 99, not 70, not 40 percent. I pay 100 percent. You hear me? I say I pay 100 percent."

And he did, not only to Landauer and Company but to each single creditor. It was from that crisis that he built a phenomenal credit rating that stretched with the years. His tenacious trust in the other man's character was reflected in the honor he had for his own.

* * *

Once an Italian fruit peddler came to his house. He was a small, weary man and humble. "Please Mr. Bragarnick," he said. "I hear you help people. You don't know me, but my horse died and my wagon is full with fruit, vegetables. Another horse costs $30."

Bragarnick said, "So why don't you buy another horse?"

The peddler said "To buy a horse needs money."

For a silent moment Bragarnick looked into the man's face. Then he reached into his pocket, counted out the bills, and turning away, briskly walked off without a word. Emily Post and Harry Bragarnick assuredly don't see eye to eye on the etiquette of gracious departure from a guest.

The peddler, for a split second, stared at the fast-retreating back and then yelled, "Hey Mr. Bragarnick! Wait! You don't know my name even. You don't know where I live."

Bragarnick stopped in his tracks. Slowly he turned and looked into the Italian peddler's face. Then he smiled. "You know my name? You know where I live? You needed money, you come to me? No? Is right or no? All right, if you wanting to pay, you'll find me again. If you don't want to pay then why should I know where you live?"

The Good Deed Man, Part 2
From the *Wisconsin Jewish Chronicle*, May 14, 1948.

One of the early walk-outs right after the 1929 crash was that of the Phoenix Hosiery mills.

The wage cuts that had to be effected by Phoenix were hitting the full fashion knitters, but in the walk-out all 1,650 employees cleared the plant in a sympathy move.

Love! Laugh! Panic!

It wasn't a mean quarrel. Everybody had always liked "The Old Man," Herman Gardner, who was the president then, and though unfortunately he wasn't around much any more because of poor health, the workers were sure everything was going to be all right. This was quite true, except that during the five or six dozen conferences that ensued things just weren't getting settled. The workers stood about the plant, hundreds deep, watching with interest the fancy imported labor experts, the lawyers and labor leaders come and go.

Joe Padway, who only a few months ago passed away, was the lawyer for the A.F.L. He was standing at the window of the vice-president's office, Theodore Friedlander. Joe himself told me about this because he felt it was the best proof how "an ounce of humanity is worth a world of wisdom."

Joe said that out there in the crowd he saw a path suddenly open wide. The thin, smiling face of Harry Bragarnick appeared. Bragarnick, it seemed, couldn't wait for things to get settled. He was a Phoenix customer and needed stock for his small store.

Padway saw how the workers were grinning and joking with Bragarnick. He could hear from outside, the good-natured yells, "Hya Mister B, long time no see." . . . One foreman stopped him to shake hands. A thin girl screamed, "Listen gang, who's all right? Bragarnick's all right." The rest laughed, but inside the vice-president's office Joe Padway muttered, "Well, I'll be darned." He hurried his short, thick bulk swiftly to the door. "Mister Bragarnick. Harry Bragarnick," he shouted. "Bring Bragarnick in here. We need him, not any militia."

* * *

And need him they did. The dispute was soon settled. The papers were full of it, but how he did it no one quite knows. Bragarnick, it seemed, settled disputes in no way that was listed in any strike conciliator's manual. Early in the game some of the conferees heard him say "mensh" for mention. "Be so kindly" when he meant be so kind. "The same I" and "What is me to do." They wondered how in glory this guy was going to put across a single idea with his cockeyed speech. But they didn't wonder long.

Bragarnick commanded the situation with his personality. It is truly a personality that seems to blaze from a frail body. And while he shrugged off rules of grammar as "small things," he was gravely swift, tough and insistent that justice, frankness and decent attitudes had to prevail.

When he was asked how he did it, he shrugged violently.

"Me? I didn't do nothing. Only is plain, a business like a home. When the husband and wife quarrels, then the maid she will steal. You understand? Is the same way in a business. Must be harmony or it falls to pieces." He shook his fist in the air and his voice rang loud. "Anyways, can't show to God you a coward. When you got right . . . then fight, fight like a lion. But if no, if you got wrong, even one percent not sure, then no money, no words, can help you be right."

The University of Michigan Department of Economics wrote and asked would he please outline his plans to the approach of strike problems. Bragarnick laughed. "Plans? What plans? Pfah! Is only human nature, that's is all."

* * *

After the Phoenix settlement, he swung into action, in earnest, as a potent, non-professional strike arbitrator. For several years he took a hand in the destinies of thousands of workers throughout Milwaukee and Wisconsin.

He helped to settle a whole slue of minor labor disputes and a few major ones. There was the Fried-Ostermann strike wherein the company had a court fight with the Amalgamated Clothing Workers' Union; the motion picture operators' union; the junk peddlers association; and most novel of all, the threatened strike of alimony delinquents in the county jail who were demanding a new hearing.

One company's problem bothered him a lot. This was the Metropolitan Life Insurance's system of charging cancellations on the policies against new business of the agents. This system frequently placed agents in the company's debt to the tune of thousands of dollars, and it was some of these agents who came to Bragarnick for help in settling their troubles. They asked him to intercede for them with the company's officials.

He spared no expense to do what he could. I myself saw telephone bills that ran into several hundred dollars for long distance calls. I know that he made at least one trip to New York to see Leroy Lincoln, the Metropolitan Life Insurance president. A strike . . . If there would have been one . . . was quashed in the making by elimination of the cancellation feature.

* * *

Just for the record, Mister B's technique of strike-settlement is quite plain, and shamelessly basic. He appeals to a man's reason through his nose and his mouth as well as his ears. First he would call the strike leaders to his home for a conference. Right off there would be beer and cigars. And then just light, aimless talk. While talking they would smell coffee, freshly cooking, wafting from the kitchen.

There was always at least one of the principals who would get fidgety and annoyed. Bragarnick was "wasting time" and why didn't he "get going?" Bragarnick always brushed it off. "You in a big hurry?" he would say ironically. "You got something better you should be doing? It's is all right. We'll straighten around together. Be sure."

Soon, when Bragarnick thought the men were sufficiently relaxed, then he was ready to "straighten around together."

He would rise, walk to the center of the room and stand, dramatically silent. With his blue eyes keen, his face sharply etched with lines and his mouth and chin set, the "Impartial Arbitrator" would begin a story.

"Boys, I'll tell you a little story from a fight in the street," he would begin with an expressive gesture. "You understand it's like this. Maybe there is two men fighting on the street with their coats off . . . like so." He would jerk his coat half off. "They are mad; they both got right and they punch hard, rough, bang, bang. Then while they fighting, two other men comes along and one he hollers, 'Give it to him good.' The second one he civilized a little bit. So, that's is human nature. In strikes, you understand," he would say, "in strikes is the same. Both got right a little bit. Both got wrong a little bit. You go in with fight, but is necessary to come out friends. Always there is room for peace. Fifty percent is friendliness, the other fifty percent, well, we'll straighten around together. So all right boys, let's us go to the table."

That phrase, "Let's us go to the table" was a clarion call. He led the way. It was almost like a battle march, except, instead of leading to the field, it led to his dining room table.

* * *

Bragarnick, it seemed, had an absolute instinct for seizing the right moment for airing strike grievances. There was always one rigid condition: discussion must open at his dining table. Why, no one is quite sure, except that the table had food and drink on it, and it is natural for a man to nibble if the stuff is right there. Besides, it is hard to stay burned up with the other guy when you have to say "Please pass the pickles" with a mouthful of corned beef.

Shortly after a strike was settled a check usually came in the mail, either from the union or the company or both. Each time the money would be accompanied by a letter to the effect that it was

". . . a slight token of our appreciation for your aid in settling our problem . . ."

The first few times it happened Bragarnick sent the checks back. "They make a mistake," he indignantly said. "Bragarnick works for men not for money." But after awhile, he would keep the check. But it bought no fancy cane or handsome tailored suits. As soon as the check arrived, he would cash it, divide it three ways, sending one part to a Catholic charity, one part to the Protestant charity and the third part to a charity of his own faith, the Jewish one.

#

Chapter 15

"You Have Such a Pretty Face"

"Childhood is what you spend the rest of your life trying to overcome."
—Sandra Bullock in the movie *Hope Floats*

"One hundred seventeen pounds," the school nurse intoned. My heart dropped to the toes of my saddle shoes. My cheeks burned. How could I weigh so much? As I stepped off the scale, I heard a shuffle outside the Health Room door and swung around to look. A short boy with big hair darted down the hall. I knew instantly who it was. "Harry Hinkle." He had stolen out of our classroom to find out how much my best friend, "Sally," and I weighed.

Every September at Cumberland School the ritual took place. The school nurse would weigh and measure us, then broadcast the results in a megaphone voice, and our teacher would record them in a notebook. I meekly submitted to this invasion of my privacy. But in fifth grade, Sally and I discovered we weighed multiple pounds more than the other girls. We suffered the titters, the humiliation. On the first day of sixth grade, we begged our teacher to let us go to the Health Room privately. She agreed, but what good did it do? Harry Hinkle was already announcing our weights to the whole class.

Growing up did not go well for me. I had begun to develop years earlier than the other girls. When I was eight, Mother made me a clingy dress in pink and rose wool. What was she thinking? Already little hills of breasts had sprouted on my chest. Whenever she forced me to wear the dress, I hunched over, curling my shoulders forward and looking like the earliest known case of osteoporosis.

Billy, the teenage boy next door, unwittingly came to my rescue. I was wearing the horrid dress to visit the grandparents one Sunday afternoon. Just before we piled into our DeSoto sedan, Billy leaned out his kitchen window and called me over. "I've got something wonderful to tell you," he said. When I trotted over and looked up at him, thrilled by the attention, he dumped a pitcherful of cold water on my head. Icy waves soaked my braids and sent arctic splashes into my mouth and ears. Blotches of water spread over the pink wool like amoebas. Mother gasped, "Your dress—it's ruined!" She turned to scold Billy, but by then he had disappeared from the window. I ran upstairs to change, my ego only a little wounded. Mostly, I felt triumphant. I knew I'd never have to put on that miserable dress again.

My days weren't totally preoccupied with my unwelcome blossoming body. This was 1943, and our Milwaukee suburb of Whitefish Bay woke up every morning dedicated to winning World War II. We filled up our small backyard with a Victory Garden: lettuce, corn, carrots, and onions. We made balls of string and tinfoil; we flattened cans. I proudly carried $18.75 to school in a cookie tin to buy a $25-dollar savings bond. Mother quit shopping at a bakery with a German name. "They're anti-Semitic," she said.

Uncle Robert was an Air Force major, on leave, coming to visit in three days. Mother spoke about him in hushed, worried tones. He flew in airplanes over India, taking pictures. *Of what?* I wondered. On the big day, Uncle Robert filled our modest living room with his powerful, broad physique and khaki uniform. The gold oak leaves glinted on his shoulders. I stood before him in fright, my neck stretching as I strained to look up at his formidable presence. I sang the song I'd been practicing all week. "Off we go, into the wild blue yonder, flying high into the sky….Nothing can stop the Army Air Corps."

All through the war, my brother and I heard a different refrain at the kitchen table: Mother urging us to be members of the

Clean Plate Club. "Starving children in Europe would love your liver with onions."

"Good!" I retorted. "Send it to them!"

"Don't get smart," Mother warned. But the message was clear to John and me. Eat all your food whether you liked it or not, whether you were still hungry or not.

On V-J Day the war ended, but my body's war against my psychological well-being was just beginning. In the spring of fifth grade, at age ten, I got my period. Misery engulfed me.

"It's okay, dear," Mother said in a soothing voice, wiping blood off my legs with a damp towel. "You're blossoming early. Aunt Lucy did too."

"Oh, great," I said. "Aunt Lucy has white hair. Does that mean I'm going to get white hair by the time I'm twelve?"

Surely, I was the only girl in the universe to get my period that early. A new proper noun forced itself into my vocabulary: Kotex. And the mechanics of it! Mother had failed to warn me about the strange pads, so thick and uncomfortable; the elastic belts with their metal claws to hold the tabs. But how could she have warned me? It was just as much a shock to her as it was to me.

To make matters worse, Sally moved away. Life was conspiring against me. My weight gain began in earnest, stealthily, half-pound by half-pound. Mother took me shopping for a new dress to wear to our temple Chanukah party. The fitting room at Gimbel's set the stage for fresh embarrassment. Chubbette dresses were the only ones that fit. Mother's full lips pursed together as she tried to control her exasperation. *She* perfectly fit the song "Five Foot Two, Eyes of Blue" and had extremely slender but shapely legs. Aunt Lucy and Aunt Dorothy had the exact same legs. I knew what was going through Mother's mind. By a quirk of genetic fate, I had inherited the pear shapes of the zaftig women on my father's side.

Ironically, eating well spelled success for my family. My parents struggled through the Depression like everyone else. (Mother once told me, "Being poor is no fun.") The word *cholesterol* was coined way back in 1894, but in the mid-Forties who'd ever heard of it or its heavy meaning? Today my brother and I joke about the five food groups at our house: meat, potatoes, bread, gravy, and dessert. Oh, we ate vegetables and salad, but the emphasis was on the other stuff.

At about the same time, Mother decided I should take my glasses off for any formal photographs. I've worn them since age ten, I'm super-near-sighted and I've always considered my glasses my friends. Obviously, Mother objected. So all the formal pictures, including my high school yearbook and college freshman book, do not look like the real me. I never protested out loud. Mother the authoritarian didn't allow much of that. Or maybe she would have if I'd tried harder and more often.

By eighth grade I had reached my full height of five-foot-four. I was the tallest and heaviest girl in my class, but not without aspirations. Mother was a journalist, so I wanted to be editor-in-chief of my junior high newspaper. Students had to campaign for the job. Mother couldn't wait to help me. She created a *shmoo* out of a white sheet and pillow stuffing. With a shape somewhere between a snowman and bowling pin, it was a remarkable copy of the *shmoos* in Al Capp's comic strip, *Li'l Abner*. A *shmoo* could be your friend or you could eat it; either way it was happy. I hefted mine from classroom to classroom. "If you vote for me," I campaigned, "your school paper will be all things to all students, just like a *shmoo*." I won.

Mother's passion for helping us backfired on Halloween. Little John returned home in tears after trick-or-treating. The neighbor kids had recognized his devil costume for what it really was: gray Dr. Denton pajamas that Mother had dyed red. Yes indeed. Dr. Dentons with feet and a drop seat that fastened with rubber buttons. Even her expertly fashioned horns and pitchfork tail hadn't impressed the other kids.

But two months later, the Halloween debacle faded into oblivion. On a below-zero January night, a calamity beyond our worst nightmares struck our house. John and I were home alone at five o'clock. John was in the basement playing with his new chemistry set. Mother pulled into the driveway, returning from a short jaunt to the library. She walked in the back door and cried, "I smell smoke." Rushing down the basement stairs, she yelled up to me: "Rosemary, call the fire department!"

"That's silly," I retorted. But then I saw the smoke, thick curls rising out of the kitchen wall—and at the bottom of the stairs, Mother trying to beat out the flames with a broom.

My father, driving home from work that bitter night, turned onto our street and spotted the fire engines up ahead. With a shock he realized they were at our house. Hours later, the four of us stood shivering and weeping amid the wreckage. Smoke, soot, and water damage surrounded us, with gaping holes in the walls where the firemen had hacked through to locate the source of the fire. Poor John bawled and bawled. In his ten-year-old's sputtered words, he told us what had happened. Playing with his chemistry set, he had thrown away a cotton ball soaked in a chemical, tossing it into a bushel basket filled with old newspapers. The cotton ball ignited the papers. The flames shot straight up through the walls to the attic.

Mother and Daddy tried to console him with hugs and reassurances that they loved him. But the truth lay unspoken: our parents were to blame. Neither one had thought to supervise their little son and teach him chemistry set safety.

Homeless for four months. Well, not really. But "home" became a house we borrowed. My psychiatrist father had a patient who spent the winter in Florida. He invited us to live in his huge English Tudor on Lake Drive while our house was under repair. What generosity—and how scary. The house reeked of an emotional chill. The nights my parents went out, I wanted to shout "Don't go! Don't leave us alone!" Babysitting John made me feel so vulnerable. The cavernous kitchen echoed with stainless steel, dark wood, and slate. Did anybody ever cook in here? *Our* cabinets had bright Pennsylvania Dutch scenes painted by Mother and her artist friend. *Our* breakfast nook had a sign on the wall created by Daddy: "Silence" in four languages and four colors, to remind John not to talk and laugh so loud. (It never did any good, of course.) The bedroom assigned to me belonged to the wife. This alone bummed me out. Separate rooms for the mother and father? Then I discovered that the wife was an invalid. I hated sleeping in her hospital bed, high off the floor, with its stiff, white antiseptic sheets and spread. Next to the bed hung a braided cord with a tassel for summoning servants.

I begged Mother to go back to our house and retrieve my own pink chenille spread with its soft little tufts. But that's when I found out she'd had to throw it away—along with so much of our family's stuff; the cleaners couldn't get the smoke smell out.

We were reading "The Gold Bug" in English class, and our assignment was to play detective and decipher the code. For the life of me, I couldn't figure it out. But I truly did feel like a character out of Edgar Allen Poe.

As an escape, I ate. Midway through freshman year of high school, I had gained twenty-five pounds. At eleven o'clock one night, as my parents were locking up, I threw myself into a kitchen chair, drew my feet up under me, and mumbled into my knees: "Nobody likes me."

"Why not?" Mother demanded.

"I don't know."

Her instant solution: "We'll give a tea!"

A tea for the popular girls who hated me. They all accepted the invitation, don't ask me why. Mother broke her neck to make the tea beautiful. And it was. Her *pièce de résistance* was rosettes. For a whole day before the tea, she stood at the kitchen counter dipping a long-handled cast-iron flower into batter and then hot fat. Gently, she nudged each golden-brown rosette out of the gizmo onto a china platter and dusted each one with powdered sugar. Mother tried so hard to get the popular girls to change their minds and like me. Nothing changed.

I consoled myself by haunting the kitchen at odd hours and secretly wolfing down leftover rosettes.

Love! Laugh! Panic!

My high school had a stellar academic record: sending 94 percent of its students on to college. When I was a freshman, I told our World History teacher that I had gotten Plato's *The Republic* out of the library. He looked pleased. "I'll help you," he said. But four pages in, I lost patience. I was too busy reading *Forever Amber*. It's a seventeenth-century historical romance about a pregnant, penniless teenager who grows up to become the favorite mistress of Charles II, the Merry Monarch. To me, the most thrilling passage came at the beginning, when Amber naively undid the top buttons of her blouson at a carnival to impress a tall, dark stranger. Next I dug into *Knock on Any Door*, about a sexy boy my age in gang-ridden Chicago. Mother discovered it in my room and promptly threw it down the garbage chute. I marched to the library and returned *The Republic*. Next, in a fit of excitement, I trotted all the way to a drugstore on Hampton Road and bought another copy of *Knock on Any Door*—being smart enough this time to hide it under my pillow. Lucky for me, Camp Pinemere was in the North Woods, where Mother couldn't censor my reading. That's where I spent five summers. One of my cabinmates got hold of *The Amboy Dukes*, a novel filled with hot, hinted-at sex and violent young hoodlums. The seven of us girls crowded around to read the one forbidden copy. But unlucky me, I was the slowest reader. I only got through the top half of each page.

Girls didn't wear pants to school in 1950—only skirts and dresses. The girls' dean was a white-haired spinster, who decided to give us some morality instructions. "Don't ever wear patent leather shoes. Your underwear will be reflected in the shoes' shiny surface." Mother giggled when I told her. "Not possible," she said. Nevertheless, I waited years before buying patent leather pumps.

Whitefish Bay High had an indoor heated pool. In early spring, my parents attended my one and only swim meet. I won the first place blue ribbon for the breast stroke. That night, a neighbor came over to congratulate me. Seated cross-legged on the couch, I basked in his praise. But after he left, World War III exploded in our living room.

Mother loomed over me and screamed: "All the other girls looked like sylphs. My daughter looked like a hippopotamus!"

Blaze assumed he was being scolded. He slunk off to the dining room and hid under the buffet. *Maybe I should run away,* I thought. *Then Mother can adopt a daughter who's thinner and doesn't wear glasses.* Instead, I ran up to my room and slammed the door. Two days later, Mother marched me into the office of Dr. Cooper, an internist and family friend. I assumed he didn't like me, because of what happened when we'd visited the Coopers a few weeks before. I chose a small fancy chair to sit on, anchored my saddle shoes on the cross-rung, and promptly cracked it in half.

The doctor put me on a 1,000-calorie-a-day diet. My after-school snack was one glass of skim milk, which tasted like chalky water, and a piece of fruit. He called to find out how I was doing.

Choking back sobs, I wailed, "I'm hungry."

He laughed, probably in retaliation for my breaking his antique chair.

On the severe regimen, I quickly dropped the twenty-five pounds. But oddly enough, my psychiatrist father did not explore the psychological source of my overeating. What was food compensating for? But there were no child psychiatrists in Milwaukee in 1950. Perhaps Dad wanted to send me for therapy, but knew of no professional he could trust. By the end of the summer, every single one of those lost twenty-five pounds had found its way back to my hips and legs.

But I hated being fat. It colored my social life—ruining my stature with the popular girls and turning off the boys I had crushes on. I still got a few dates and had girlfriends: highly intelligent, nice ones, who seemed not to care about my weight. Still, I kept clinging to the fringes of the popular set. Sitting at my dressing table, the mirror reflected a basically pretty face, although rather too round; hazel eyes, tawny and flexed with gold; and thick, naturally curly brown hair. My original largish nose now had a significant bump. A few years before, a neighbor girl hit me on the nose with a roller skate because I had said something nasty to her.

Love! Laugh! Panic!

At this moment in my life Mother issued two new obnoxious decrees. I would henceforth call Dad "Father." "It's more dignified," she said. Truth is, she got the idea from a rich friend. Second, she agreed to buy me new clothes, but on one condition: "You have to wear a girdle." We drove downtown to Dreier Meier, the lingerie store. I knew I was doomed the moment we entered; there wasn't a single customer under the age of forty. I became the only fifteen-year-old on the planet to wear a girdle. But not just a Spandexy control thing. This girdle resembled a medieval chastity belt. It extended from my hips to just under my breasts, had a long zipper, and was so stiff it could have stood straight up on the floor by itself. The stiffness came from its vertical plastic stays that cut into my ribs. Yes, the girdle did make me look a lot trimmer, but at what cost?

Over the next two years, I tried to reform my body in my own way. I bought a box of square caramel candies called Ayds. Eating one before a meal was supposed to suppress your appetite. But they tasted so good! I ate the whole boxful in three days and hid the waxy wrappers under my mattress. The cleaning lady turning my mattress reported the stash to Mother. A movie magazine ad lured me into buying a wide rubber wrap. "Wear it for three hours and Presto! Inches will melt off your hips and waist." All it did was make me sweat. Eleven dollars I lost! But no inches. I bought other seductive magazines. They all promised to help me. "Trim and Firm Your Body in 21 Days." "Cut Calories and Get Gorgeous." But a half-hour of reading only made me feel betrayed. For every article on how to lose weight I found at least three describing fattening dishes, complete with recipes and color pictures, that would make Pavlov salivate in his grave. In *Family Circle*, sandwiched between two articles on proper eating habits, were six gravy recipes and five color pages on "Luscious Coffee Cakes."

Senior year in high school I got my driver's license, and Mother generously lent me her Plymouth convertible to shop downtown on my own. Big mistake. I always ended up at Gimbel's bakery counter, where I'd buy six maple Danish or a box of Fairy

Food: large cubes of meringue covered in dark chocolate. One evening we had a visitor, Aunt Molly. We were all chatting pleasantly in the living room, when Blaze came padding down the stairs, carrying something unfamiliar in his mouth. *Oh, no! Earth, swallow me up now!* Blaze settled his shaggy bulk on the rug in front of Aunt Molly and proceeded to lick his prize: a hunk of Fairy Food, purloined from the box hidden under my bed.

But I didn't really have to buy any of it. A sweet tooth ran in the family, and Mother not only baked divinely, but kept the house full of candy and pastry. She and Father could nibble, but I had no self-control. Father received a holiday gift from a patient: a ten-pound chocolate bar, two inches thick. When my parents went out for the evening, I took a hammer and screwdriver and hacked off large chunks. To this day, I ponder why my parents allowed so many sweets in our house. Was Mother catering to Father? Or was she subconsciously sabotaging my efforts to lose weight?

Grandma Elizabeth brooded over her oldest grandchild's figure and let me know. "You have such a pretty face," she often said. But hinting wasn't enough. As reinforcement, she paid, in advance, for six sessions at a so-called weight-loss center. Grandma had learned of it over her weekly canasta game. My parents had never heard of it, but sent me anyway. On my first visit, an unsmiling burly matron ushered me in. I fully expected her to shout "*Achtung!*" The session consisted of three parts. First she weighed me. Then I had to strip naked and get massaged (covered with a towel). Last, I got hosed down. Yes! I had to step naked into a narrow tiled room about fifteen feet long. The matron stood at the other end and sprayed a harsh stream of water on me for ten minutes (maybe less, but to me it seemed an eternity). Between the insensitivity, the humiliation, and the total lack of logic in this program, I fervently wished to die right then and there—or, preferably, that the matron would. I never went back, even though Grandma had already paid for another session. My parents and Grandma never found out, because I became an accomplished dissembler without actually coming out with a lie. I merely remained at my after-school job for an extra two hours (eating ice cream drumsticks in the lounge) to make it look like I'd gone to the weight-loss Gestapo.

Aside from that wicked place, senior year came out pretty well. I became co-editor-in-chief of our school paper and got accepted to Smith College. Mother had been encouraging me to apply to Ivy League schools since I was fourteen. I had no idea why. Did she want to bask in the prestige? Or did she want her daughter to be a thousand miles away? The only downside to Smith was the requisite uniform: Bermuda shorts. Mother took me to buy them. I slumped against the fitting room wall, a barrel in wool plaid. We bought three expensive pairs in a preppy Ivy League Milwaukee shop. I never once put them on.

Shortly after I arrived at Smith, in the fall of 1953, I saw girls walking around sobbing. Dylan Thomas had died. I'd never heard of him, and when the girls told me he was a revered Welsh poet, I couldn't believe it. Students crying over the death of a poet? I must be in the right place! The brainy atmosphere crackled everywhere on campus, especially as we freshmen sat on our beds and debated literature and political philosophy.

My social life proved less exhilarating at this wooded, isolated campus. Our dates came on weekends from the surrounding men's colleges: Amherst, Yale, Harvard, Williams, Trinity. There was no such thing as a casual cup of coffee between classes. For me, boys were not mere mortals. Dates meant visitations from young gods on pedestals. Boys actually terrified me, perhaps because I'd always felt somewhat in awe of my distinguished father. In my entire college career, I never made even one male *friend*. And let me not forget my excess weight. I'm sure it stunted my social life.

Phone calls were Events. Each of the four floors of Gardiner House had one phone booth—in the hall. Someone would answer and yell, "Rosemary! Long distance!" A long distance call was special and expensive. On my parents' once-a-week calls, Father asked me, "How come I never hear the last names of any of the boys you date?" Easy answer. I hardly ever had second dates. But he must have known that. Mother remained tactfully silent.

One friend on my floor, "Roxy," had a boyfriend named "Carl." He drove up to see her on weekends in a nifty little sports car with the top down. They were having a stormy love affair, Roxy told me. Since I had never had a boyfriend of any kind, this didn't sound so bad. Flopping on my bed, she talked about him and said things like "I want Carl to undress me." I could only imagine. One day they had an argument on the lawn in the center of the Quad. Their angry shouts reverberated on the bricks of our dorms. We all opened our windows and leaned out to listen and watch. Suddenly, Carl jumped into his car and sped off, circling around, heading toward the archway out. Roxy started running diagonally across the vast lawn to intercept him, shouting "Carl, Carl!" Just before the archway, he braked and she jumped in beside him. Off they drove. I thought this was the most romantic thing I'd ever seen in my life. Why didn't I have a boyfriend from Yale I could have melodramatic fights with? Moodily, I knew the answer. I was too fat.

I was so socially naïve that I usually had no idea what was going on in Gardiner House. It wasn't until our twenty-fifth reunion that I found out the girl across the hall from me had had two abortions by her sophomore year. One senior, "Irene," had a hunk of a boyfriend. Dexter, dark-haired, powerfully built. Abruptly, Irene started dating a wimpy, pale guy with narrow shoulders. After graduating *summa cum laude,* she married him. We freshmen were dismayed, and rightly so. A month after her wedding, she sent us a postcard. "I took twenty-two books on my honeymoon—and read them all."

My freshman roommate came from Ohio. Her mother often sent her large boxes of sweets, especially enormous frosted cinnamon buns. When I studied alone in our room, I sometimes pulled out her box from under her bunk bed and stole one, scarfing it down quickly not to be discovered. But a few months later, out of the blue, Nancy said, "Many of the cinnamon buns are missing. I know who took them, Rosie." With a blank look I answered, "You do?" She had the good graces to drop the subject. Five decades later, at our fiftieth reunion, we were ambling through the art museum together and I finally faced her. "Nancy, I have a confession to make. I was the one who stole your cinnamon buns." She looked at me quizzically and laughed. "I don't even remember." Still, it was a load of my chest. Now that's an awfully long time to carry such guilt.

Home for the summer, my family and I sat in the living room together and watched *Twenty-One*. I promptly fell in love with the gorgeous, brainy contestant Charles Van Doren. He was engaged to a Jewish girl, and Aunt Lucy read my mind. "Oh, Rosemary, you should have been her." He brought drama to the isolation booth—tall body tense, eyes closed, as if he were squeezing the answers out of his brain with great effort. But as we watched, Father just shook his head. "I don't know. He looks awfully professional to me." Prophetic, brilliant Father. Charles Van Doren turned out to be a fraud: he'd been briefed ahead of time with every answer. Ironically, he likely would have known every answer without cheating. He lost his teaching job at Columbia and disillusioned flocks of students like me.

As a Government major, I was accepted into Smith's Junior Year Abroad program in Geneva, Switzerland. I had no big interest in Government, but Smith didn't have a program abroad back then for English majors. I would've majored in Sanskrit if necessary.

Time to pack. All the other girls were taking suitcases. But not me, not with Mother in charge. She located a second-hand wardrobe trunk, complete with hangers and little drawers, like I was Zsa Zsa Gabor with personal porters to heft the bulky thing. This was 1955. We had heard—who knows where?—that sanitary napkins were hard to come by on the Continent. When all my stuff was packed, Father, Mother, and I stuffed Kotex pads into every nook and cranny of my trunk. Surprise! I discovered you could get them in every drugstore in France and Switzerland.

We spent six weeks in Paris living with families to get up to speed in French. I have no facility for languages. Despite five years of French, I arrived in Paris a deaf-mute. I could neither speak nor understand the language. All my classmates were doing fine. Finally, after a month, it clicked; I "got it." Off we went for the school year at the University of Geneva and Graduate Institute of International Studies. Meanwhile, from the Eiffel Tower to the Swiss Alps to the island of Malta, I ate—and overate. In the bathtub of my Swiss "family," I secretly munched Lindt chocolate bars. At Oktoberfest in Berne, I nibbled marzipan pigs' heads filled with cream.

One night I received a trans-Atlantic phone call from Father. Mother was sick. Not flu-sick. Gravely ill with stomach trouble. That explained why she hadn't sent me a letter in two weeks. She was so faithful that I'd had a haunted feeling of something not right. Mother had had nine operations in her life and another one was scheduled. Father brought me home from Geneva for a week. Twenty-two hours each way by plane. No jets in 1956. I felt sorry for the stewardesses. They were cheerful but exhausted as they worked the entire route with stops in Paris; Shannon, Ireland; Gander, Newfoundland; and finally New York, where I changed planes for Milwaukee. Mother's tenth surgery was "exploratory," during which the surgeon merely closed her up and said she had four months to live. Father told John and me that a tumor was encircling the aorta in her abdomen. He didn't use the word *cancer*. In 1956 cancer was a hush-hush subject. But that's what it was.

I got back to Geneva in time for final exams, most of which were oral and in French. My friend Adelle lent me her notes from the classes I had missed in International Law, but somehow I couldn't get the material through my head. I was still airplane-lagged and upset about Mother. In our oral exams, the deal was this. The professor sat behind his desk, which had an assortment of folded slips of paper on it. You took one; it had one question on it. That was your entire exam and, in fact, your entire grade. You were sent out to the waiting room for twenty minutes to scribble a few notes, and then you returned to the dreaded inner sanctum. I stood in front of Professor Guggenheim, a distinguished international lawyer, and stumbled over a few words, unable to recall much of Adelle's notes.

He eyed me sternly and asked me in French, "Mademoiselle, what *do* you know?"

"*Rien,*" I said. Nothing. I was too scared and too tongue-tied to tell him the truth. He flunked me. The director of our group later spoke to him on my behalf, explaining why I'd been away. Professor Guggenheim changed my grade from an F to a D so I would at least pass the course.

So I passed my junior year. Funny thing. The only time I ever made Dean's List in my four Smith years was the first semester in Geneva, when I wrote two term papers in French. One was forty pages on U.S. diplomacy during the American Civil War. The other, a forty-five-minute oral report comparing the Yugoslav constitutions of 1939 and 1945. That course was Constitutional Law, and on the first day thirty students showed up. The professor told us that the oral report was it: our entire semester assignment. Next class: only six of us showed up. The rest fled and dropped the course.

I owed my success in those research projects to Mother. She lent me her Royal portable typewriter, on which she had French accent marks installed just for me. And in my clunky trunk I brought along the famous Chanukah gift, *The Lincoln Library of Essential Information*. I think of the endless midnights when I had a resource to look a fact up.

Recently, I described my curriculum to a friend, and he innocently threw me a curve by asking, "What *were* the differences between those two Yugoslav constitutions?"

"Jeez," I said, my cheeks burning. "Who knows? That was fifty-six years ago." Ouch. The penalty for bragging.

On Father's orders, I chucked my summer travel plans and went straight home. Getting there was something else. I sailed from Southampton on the *Mauritania*, the Cunard Line. Student class, quite an adventure. Top bunk in a cabin with three friendly English girls. A storm on the North Sea, the ship rocking and pitching for four days. Taking a bath in salt water with a board across the tub and a metal pan of fresh water on it for my face. Boozy Irish immigrants sitting on the floor in steerage, mournfully singing Irish songs.

Right after boarding, a beautiful surprise awaited me in my cabin: a present for my twenty-first birthday from my close friends in the Smith group. They had arranged it from Geneva, a large bucket decorated with Toulouse-Lautrec paintings. Inside it was a bottle of champagne and a coffee-table book, *Seventeenth-Century Dutch Art*. We had taken the course at the university. It's still my favorite period of art.

I arrived home to take care of Mother for the summer. A hellish time was had by all.

My bedridden mother looked so emaciated and hollow-cheeked that her horn-rimmed glasses dwarfed her delicate face. She placed her weak arms around me, then lay back and issued her critique. "You've gained so much weight! And the neckline on that dress—it's not flattering."

It's your fault, you bought it for me, I wanted to say, but I swallowed the words.

That whole summer I faced the challenge of creating meals that Mother could tolerate. It would have been easier to climb the Matterhorn barefoot.

I trooped up the stairs with her dinner tray and set it on the bed, where she sat propped up against the pillows. I prayed she'd savor my offering, or at least be able to keep it down. She took two bites and pushed the tray away, then eyed me as I stood beside the bed.

"Rosemary, what's the matter? You look so mean."

I wanted to explain, but couldn't. My emotions bubbled in a bottle—corked so tight that I couldn't articulate my feelings to anyone, even myself. How could I confess to Mother that, each day, I flailed in a quicksand of frustration and despair, unable to fix her a meal that she could, literally, stomach. One evening, Father, John, and I stood anxiously around her bed. She was sitting up, doubled over in pain, when she cried out, "God, let me die." John and I left the room in tears and went down to the kitchen. A few minutes later, Father joined us. "Mother apologizes for her outburst." I think back on that scene, so unlikely to happen today. Because today we are taught to confront cancer, to talk about it, to enlist the help of a hospice. Mother never uttered the word and neither did we. I was in denial. Instead of leaving the room, why didn't we put our arms around her and talk about the future, or the future that wouldn't be? The ache stays with me to this day.

The unbearable frustration of not being able to help or soothe. It was the same frustration I'd felt at camp when I was twelve, 260 miles from home in Minocqua, Wisconsin. For several days in July, I'd had a premonition that something was wrong at home. The dread lurked inside me even when I was canoeing, playing volleyball, and picking blueberries. One night I dreamt that our house was on fire and I was upstairs in the hall, flames roaring, shooting high. My parents' bedroom was across the hall. Mother was inside and I couldn't get to her. At the end of August, when I returned home from camp, Father confessed that, in July, Mother had gone to a hospital in Chicago for yet another operation.

Ironically, the symbolic fire in my dream took place only six months before the actual fire in our house.

Another time when Mother was ill, we had a cleaning lady named "Charlotte," who came several times a week. Six feet tall and built like a forklift, she arrived each day carrying a large empty shopping bag. And each night when she left, it was full. Mother wasn't totally bedridden. Nor was she naïve. In her bare feet and nightgown, she checked out the linen closet. Belgian-lace tablecloths and matching napkins were missing. Then she checked out the "preserving cellar"—her dignified name for the basement room filled with shelves of home-canning and stuff. She placed a small scrap of paper deep in the bushel basket of apples. Two days later, the paper sat nakedly on top, with the bushel basket now only half-full. When Mother took a small turn for the better, Charlotte got fired. I felt sick in my gut at her blatant chutzpah and meanness, taking such advantage of my sick mother.

My parents' Episcopalian friends asked if they could bring "Father Lawson" to visit. "He's a lovely man, Luby, and he would like to visit because he's heard such great things about you." Father Lawson came once a week. He would chat for a few minutes, sitting in the rocking chair, and before leaving, he would stand beside the bed, and in a soft voice, he'd say a nonsectarian prayer that always seemed to soothe Mother. And tore my heart up with his gentle, kind manner. Many years later, he and his wife were on a Caribbean vacation, when they had a car accident. He was driving. His wife was killed. He never recovered, but moved to the islands as a missionary. Such a terrible, undeserved fate for a true man of God.

Mother actually had some good days. One of her younger doctors, an athletic man with a crew cut, came to check on her after a trip to Aspen, Colorado. In a strong voice, she said to him: "Sam, when I get well you'll teach me to ski." And she meant it.

One Saturday afternoon in the backyard, Father had just given instructions to Emil, our sometime gardener. Emil had been Father's patient years before at the Milwaukee County Mental Hospital and had done so well there that he got a good industrial assembly-line job and came to us occasionally on weekends to tend our small yard. He was about forty, a huge man, broad and strong, with a deep hoarse voice and craggy face. He would arrive early in the morning and Mother would offer him breakfast. "Bring it on, Mrs. Pollack!" he boomed with a wave of his hand, and seated himself in our breakfast nook, where he seemed to overwhelm the small space. Gracious Mother would fix him a large meal, later whispering to me, "He ate twelve eggs!" Emil had a staunch sense of gratitude—to my father for rescuing him from his mental illness, and to my mother for her kindness. Although he was a passionate churchgoer, he always sent us cards on Rosh Hashanah and Passover: lavish, sentimental ones. For a man who appeared rough-cut, he signed his name in surprisingly beautiful, swirling script.

On that particular Saturday, with Mother very sick in bed, our friends Bob and Grace came into the backyard looking for us; no one had answered the doorbell. They'd come to pay a sick call. Grace was a particularly affectionate woman who adored Mother.

She was also blonde. She threw her arms around Father in an expression of loving sympathy. Emil, clipping hedges, saw the hug, and a look of great distress shadowed his face. Father knew why. Emil had totally misunderstood. He assumed Father and Grace were having an affair. His loyalty to Mother was so overwhelming that he could imagine nothing else. He never came to our house again.

I yearned for the summer to be over and felt guilty for wishing it. In September I returned to Smith for my senior year. But I spent it marking time. Junior year in Europe had spoiled me, making me feel disconnected from campus life and even from my friends who had not gone abroad. I felt so worldly, so sophisticated. Fair or not, bratty or not, I couldn't wait to graduate.

Mother fought the heartbreaking fight, lasting fifteen months, not four. She died two months before my graduation, on April 1st, 1957. I could barely concentrate on my last papers and cramming for exams. Images of Mother in the hospital that final week—jaundiced, unconscious—pressed upon my brain. This was not the mother I knew or wanted to remember. The images stalked me, competing with my notes on American Foreign Policy and the UN. After my World Literature exam, an essay test, as all my exams were, the professor called me with bad news. "Rosemary, I'm sorry, but I had to give you a B. You forgot to answer the last two questions."

The night Mother died, I threw myself into a starvation diet: 600 calories a day. For her. And for myself. By graduation week, I had lost twenty-five pounds and bought two size-ten dresses. One friend said, "Rosemary, you look positively svelte!" No one had ever said that to me before.

But on graduation morning, studying myself in the mirror, I detected something strange. My once luxurious head of hair had thinned. And in the weeks ahead, something else happened. Whenever I got the slightest scratch or cut, it became infected and refused to heal normally. Two years passed before an alert doctor discovered the source of my problems: the starvation diet had triggered anemia. The anemia got pretty well controlled, but left me with permanent damage to my hair. It never regained its fullness, its luster, or its natural curls.

Still . . . today I'm happy with myself. I'm now two sizes smaller than in high school and steer a stable course. Salesladies have even called me "skinny." It's a lie, but I love it.

I wish I could boast that I've kept the pounds off without help, but that too would be a lie. In my early forties, my rocky marriage of seventeen years painfully spiraled downhill. I entered psychotherapy about the same time as my divorce and continued once a week for several years. Our precious daughter was nine. I had full custody and joked grimly with my friends that packing her lunches was turning me into a Ho-Ho freak.

Therapy helped prevent me from gaining twenty-five or thirty pounds, but it alone did not shut off the bingeing engine. Four or five times a year, I yo-yo dieted, losing and gaining ten pounds. I'd get "svelte" for a business convention and munch candy bars in the car driving home. I tried various weight-loss fads: the grapefruit diet; the water diet; shakes laced with bran. Ugh! Obviously—and I knew it was self-destructive—this was not a healthy way to live. The radical swings were punishing my body. They were also damaging my self-esteem. I often avoided, or canceled, social engagements when I was on the higher side. Just too embarrassed to go.

What finally stabilized me was the astute assessment of my primary care physician. He prescribed thyroid pills, a modest dose. They seem to be just what the doctor ordered. Once a year he requires blood work to make sure the dose is correct.

On New Year's Eve 1993 Larry and I decided to take early retirement the following September, to spend the winters in Hawaii. After a forty-year career, Larry was definitely entitled to early retirement. So I went to my Human Resources director at Westinghouse, where I was an engineering writer, and asked, "What is it called when you retire after six-and-a-half years?"

He eyed me with a flicker of amusement, and in a commanding voice, he said, "It's called quitting."

Okaaaaay.

I had nine months to lose weight so I'd be happier in shorts and bathing suits. Off to Grant City, where I bought an aerobic step that came with a "Body-Shaping" tape. I lost twelve pounds. Down a whole size in pants! But there's no free lunch. So much weight came off my face that I looked about ten years older. Well, at least five. Larry is three years older than I am, but his face is less lined. Somehow I can't go the Botox route. It scares the daylights out of me. Besides, my husband loves me the way I am. Which is a good thing, because my hair has grown thinner and thinner, and all the volumizing shampoos, conditioners, and sprays in the world aren't helping. So when we go out, I wear my new friend, Winnie the Wig. It's quite pert, but not outrageously flamboyant. Larry says I look younger! Woweeee!

I've received a lifelong dividend that I didn't expect. Flipping through family photo albums, I've discovered that, with my much thinner face, I actually look a lot like Mother. It makes me sad to think she's never seen the slender me. But then again, maybe all this time she *has* been looking down on me. I choose to believe she has—and that she approves.

Chapter 16

The Debutante

"Rosemary, I have marvelous news for you!"

This better be good. My mother was calling me at deadline time, and I was standing with the phone to my ear at the corner of the news editor's desk.

"What?"

"You're going to be making your debut!"

The hairs on the back of my neck bristled. My stomach curdled. "How do you know?"

"Because I arranged it, that's how!" Mother's voice warbled with triumph.

The teletype clacked away in the back room, rhythmic, metronomic, hypnotic. Other phones jangled. I prayed the editors and reporters were too busy to hear me. Cupping my hand around the receiver, I hissed in a half-whisper, "Mother, I don't want to make my debut."

"Don't you dare tell your father that!"

Forget it, Mother. I will too tell him. You had no right to go behind my back and do this without asking me first. That's what I wanted to say, in a loud voice that would leave no doubt. But I didn't. I'd already lost the battle.

"We'll talk about it when I get home," I mumbled and hung up.

I rushed back to my desk. I was being broken in to write radio news at WTMJ, the *Milwaukee Journal* radio station the summer before my sophomore year at Smith. Mostly I was doing clerical work, but now and then I'd be rewarded with an assignment. Working for this station felt like the center of the universe to me, a promotion from two summers as a copygirl, a gofer, on the *Milwaukee Journal*. At this moment I had moved up in the world, I was responsible for five minutes of news. A five-minute broadcast took an hour to prepare, and Mother had just wasted five of my precious minutes. I sifted through the scrolled pile of Associated Press articles hot off the teletype, shuffled through the local stories the reporters had handed me, and dug in. A Midwest train wreck. Pickpockets at the state fair. I could hardly focus without spilling my alarm and panic all over my boss's desk, but that wasn't something you did here. The clock dictated our behavior. At that moment, meeting the deadline for the five o'clock news broadcast was all that counted.

But focusing was a skill I hadn't quite mastered. "My mother is forcing me to make my debut," I blurted out to the editor-in-chief.

"Jake" raised his bald head from the copy he was editing. His pale eyes lit up with wry amusement. "Debut as in debutante? What a tragedy. We'll put it on the six o'clock news. Ivy League girl to be tortured by pampering, spoiling, and becoming queen for a night."

My face went hot. I burrowed in, typing furiously on my manual Royal, and finished the five minutes of news with time to spare. Jake studied my copy, then nodded in a rare sign of approval. "Good job. You're not entirely doomed."

Proud of myself, I climbed into my mother's sea-green DeSoto convertible, top down. Sailing through the benign traffic, I let the breeze ruffle my poodle haircut and reflected on the phone call. Crossing my mother amounted to mutiny. When I was four, she told me the story of "Naughty Nancy and Goody Two-Shoes"—a poorly disguised sermon. I was also expected to be Responsible. We lived in a duplex. One night I left my tricycle outside. The lady who lived upstairs tripped over it and tore her "white sharkskin dress," Mother said. She sent me upstairs to apologize. I was supposed to feel remorse, but all I could think of was, the lady wore a fish?

I braked for a red light and sighed. It wasn't easy to mount a rebellion against your mother on days she allowed you to borrow her convertible. Usually, I had to catch the bus at 5:30 a.m.

Whenever we tried to defy her, Mother would shout at John and me: "Show me some respect!" I always marveled at how loud her voice was and how it scared the daylights out of me. The voice just didn't go with her petite body. Tiny waist, 105 pounds. How did all that fury manage to emerge from such a slender space? Her lungs must have been the size of Lake Oconomowoc. But why was I always so scared? I was taller and heavier than Mother. She should have been the intimidated one.

My palms felt sweaty as I pulled into our driveway. Opening the screen door to the kitchen, I heard Mother on the phone in the den, chortling the news to Aunt Dorothy in Washington, D.C. And by the time she hung up I realized the generalissimo had already marshaled an armament of arguments to defeat my objections.

"Why did you do this without asking me first?" I demanded.

"Because I knew you'd say no."

"But what does Father think?" I had a pretty good idea what his opinion would be: a phony, pretentious, expensive exercise for Junior Leaguers. Which we weren't.

Mother's crystal blue eyes glinted with annoyance. "He doesn't know yet."

"I didn't think so. Why do I have to make my debut anyway? I don't even know those girls. Let's just forget the whole thing."

Mother whirled about in her swivel chair. "Rosemary, for heaven's sake, you act like this is a prison sentence. It'll be fun."

"Like what?" I asked sourly.

"There'll be lots of parties and dances given by the girls' parents."

"Gee," I sneered, "a social whirl in the metropolis of Milwaukee. Why do I have the only mother in the world who orchestrates her daughter's whole life without permission?"

"Why do I have the only daughter in the world whose sole purpose in life is to be negative? If you'd just try to think about the positive side of your debut. We'll give a tea, very elegant. Maybe I can swing it to be at one of the country clubs. And then you thirty girls will all be presented to society at the Coming Out Ball at Christmastime."

Presented to Society? Oh, my God. Suddenly I wanted to be ten again. Playing Fifty-All-Scatter after supper and hiding with cute Bobby Bingham. Playing jacks in our driveway with Joan and Gail, the sun-baked cement warming our legs. Roller skating: tightening the brackets around my shoes with the square key; the heavy wheels of my ball-bearing skates sending grinding noises on the sidewalk and a tingling sensation through my body. And Mother poking her head out the bedroom window at 7 a.m. Sunday morning. "Rosemary, go skate down the block. The racket is waking your father. It's his only day to sleep!"

Mother smelled my fear and reared out of her chair. "Rosemary, thousands of girls would give their eyeteeth to make their debut."

I frowned. "What exactly are eyeteeth, Mother?"

She pursed her cupid lips into a smile. "I don't really know. Look it up."

"Not now," I pouted.

"Yes, do it now while it's fresh."

Reluctantly, I opened the *Webster's International Dictionary* resting on its tall stand next to the desk, and flipped to the e's. "They're canine teeth in the upper jaw."

"Oh." She laughed gaily. "Well, thousands of girls would give them up." Then her expression turned dark. "Listen, young lady, I have spent the greater part of my days on the phone for months to make this possible and you are not going to sabotage it."

I stopped listening. Blah blah blah blah blah.

"Besides, it's for your own good. The perfect social vehicle for you. You'll meet so many nice, well-connected young men. Men you'd have no opportunity to meet any other way."

"No opportunity? That's pretty funny. Isn't that what you sent me to an Ivy League school for?"

Crossing her bony arms over her chest, she announced, "One thing is for sure, young lady, we didn't send you to Smith College to come home and be snippy and defiant. The subject is closed."

The debut business was Mother's grand plan for marrying me off. "Nice" and "well-connected" really translated to "a rich man from a powerful family." Of which there were many in Milwaukee, a city of about half a million, but megamillions in wealth; the families who owned the giant breweries, the factories of heavy industry, farm machinery, inboard and outboard motors. Schlitz, Pabst, Miller Brewing Company, Allis-Chalmers, Kearney & Trekker, Manpower, Evinrude Motors, and on and on.

Fresh out of arguments, I ran up to my room and slammed the door. What was this all about, really? Months ago, at a low moment, Mother had confided in me. Two long-time friends had formed a literary club. But instead of inviting her to join, they maliciously sent her an application form! Mother foolishly filled it out. They rejected her! These women were beneath her intellectually, professionally, in every way. I was horrified that she had taken the bait.

Something about this debutante business unnerved me, but at that moment I couldn't articulate what was generating my fear. Even being on the brink of my sophomore year didn't seem to help. Smith was teaching me to think, to reason. But abstractly. Somehow, writing essay exams on the political philosophies of Aristotle and John Locke just did not translate into the skill of defying my mother. I sat down on my dressing table stool, letting the skirt encircle my legs, and stared at myself in the mirror.

Where had the fear come from? When I was eight, my parents gave me my first ice skates for Chanukah. Not the double runner kind for little kids, but single blades, the real thing. I took them to school, and when the bell rang at 3:30 I ran to the skating pond, the football field frozen over. The after-school races were already in progress. I had never ice skated—ever. I shoved my feet into the skates, laced them up, and entered a race to go around the pond once. Skater after skater finished and I was still only halfway around, doggedly pushing myself forward—on my ankles. It never occurred to me to quit and I was not the least bit embarrassed. When I finally crossed the finish line, a chorus of "Yea!" and mittens clapping greeted me. At what point in my life did that gutsy third grader abandon me?

Now I was an Ivy League girl. That should have been enough to give me credibility with the other debutantes. It was only at the first party that I discovered it wasn't.

Early in July, the phone rang and a boy I'd never met invited me to the first debut party, a picnic out in the country. I had never met the girl giving it. Her kindly mother assigned him to be my date. He was blond, had a crew cut, and loved water skiing. In the car we talk stiffly, and I was relieved when we arrived.

The large rambling house sat on a piece of flat farmland with lots of grass, but no visible animals. The highlight of the picnic was a caricaturist hired to do a drawing of each of us. He set up an easel in the sunroom, with all thirty of us girls, plus our dates, crowded around, watching each gentle spoof emerge.

Standing there in my cotton dress I felt awkward, a Martian deep in the heart of White Anglo-Saxon Protestant country. WASP hair surrounded me; glossy, automatic hair that fell effortlessly on tanned shoulders. But worse, I was engulfed by a sea of slender calves and firm thighs. I was the only one at the whole picnic not wearing shorts because ever since I was fourteen, I'd looked wretched in shorts.

The artist worked away, sweeps of brush strokes here, dabs there, touches of color, flourishes of eyebrows and ponytails. Girl after girl, boy after boy, took their place in the chair to be drawn.

As the artist finished each one, the guests took their drawings and drifted outside for more ham and potato salad. My date, second last, got his drawing. I didn't. The only one who didn't. No one, not even my date, spoke up and said, "Rosemary's turn." Of course, I could have said "My turn." But I'd have died first.

What was I doing here? All the debs and all the boys had been preppies at Country Day this, University School that; they all knew each other, grew up together.

At that moment I had a defining pinpoint of illumination. I had just learned about James Joyce and his epiphanies. My English professor would have been thrilled that I was actually applying what I'd learned. This was it. In that stuffy sunroom awash with unfriendly light, I realized that I was the only public school girl there. And I was something else the other girls were not: I was Jewish. Watching the others get their caricatures drawn, a sickening thought flashed through my mind. I was the token Jew. Is that what this was all about? My mother's obsession with being accepted into Milwaukee high society?

"How was the party?" Mother asked in a chirpy trill, waiting for me to gush forth the lovely details.

"Fine." Selectively I told her about the farmhouse, the food. But not about the caricatures. Not about being the only girl there in a dress. The only overweight girl. I couldn't tell her the truth. After all, it was up to me to be a success. At school. At parties. As Mother's little debutante.

So on that painful Saturday afternoon I described my first debut event to Mother as peachy, swell, neat, fun.

"How was your date?" she compulsively inquired.

"We tolerated each other," I said as I backed out of the den and raced up to my room. Mother the journalist was an expert interviewer. Once she started grilling me I'd be dead meat.

The picnic fiasco mercifully faded from my mind as the summer gathered momentum. The heat and humidity blanketed our city sprawled along Lake Michigan. Our house hummed with laboring electric fans. The Rice Krispies tasted like they had milk in them before the milk was poured—soggy, not crunchy.

I refused to admit it to Mother, but reluctantly I began to enjoy my celebrity status. At work, my editor-in-chief and the reporters—tough, smart newsmen—seemed impressed as my name popped up *en groupe* in the society pages. And I discovered that the parties weren't so painful after all. Mostly because there were no more picnics and I actually looked quite pretty in dresses. Mother was beside herself with excitement as white linen envelopes arrived, as imposing as wedding invitations, with embossed or sometimes even engraved lettering. Inviting me to this and that formal dance.

I began to have fun. Most of the girls turned out to be pleasant, or at least courteous, and one was remarkably nice to me. My family visited hers one Sunday afternoon. The "Wallerons" lived in a hundred-year-old white house near the lake with high ceilings and a balcony overlooking the two-story foyer. "Carter" and "Evelyn" were friends of my parents. Exuberant and affectionate.

"Your father helps me so much," Evelyn confided, her arm about my shoulders. "I don't know how I'd cope without him." I listened in disbelief. No one had ever confessed to me to being one of his patients.

Carter Walleron—fortyish, lean, athletic—joked with us, then called out, "C'mere, Big Brown Dog." A sleek hound galloped into the living room and skidded on the parquet floor. Rearing on his hind legs, he rested his front paws on Carter's shoulders and licked his cheek.

"John, do you like dogs?" Carter asked my brother. John's face lit up with joy as he launched into tales of our golden retriever. He spent the rest of our visit wrestling with Big Brown Dog. Carrie took me upstairs to show me her dress for her own debut party. She was as genuine as my closest Smith friends. The private school-public school thing didn't seem important to Carrie.

On the way home, tucked into our sedan, we basked in the Walleron family warmth, which most certainly had floated out to our car and settled around us.

Mother asked me, "Did I tell you Carter is the president of 'Blue Moon Sugar'?"

"Wow," I said. We baked with it all the time. Were company presidents usually so homespun?

As the invitations to the parties arrived, Mother launched nonstop into a new topic, the dresses I'd need. The department stores just wouldn't do. No Gimbel's or Boston Store for us. It had to be Zita's, an exclusive boutique, where you bought one-of-a-kind gowns. The more she talked, the more Father's expression soured.

At Zita's, a thin, smug saleslady approached us. Her experienced eye swept over me and my hips. She disappeared and reappeared with hangers of pastel fluff. After infinite try-ons, only one dress was left. I stared at myself in the three-way mirror: a zaftig vision, as if the ballet fairies had stayed up all night stitching together sixty lime-green tutus.

"Lovely! We'll take it," Mother said. Then we settled on a peacock blue velvet with a cape neckline to make me look broader in the shoulders and narrower in the hips. This was the one for my debut tea. "They'll be taking your picture for the society page," Mother said just loud enough for the saleslady to hear. But Miss Officious didn't look impressed. She heard it a dozen times a day. Mother announced, "We're not done yet. You need a gown for the Coming Out Ball itself."

Oh, that. And I was so hoping we could put it off. The saleslady smiled for the first time. Big commission coming up. She padded away on the thick carpet and floated back out bearing an armload of pouffy white things—the required white to be Presented to Society. The gowns were all strapless and I climbed into them one by one, got zipped up, zipped down, until Mother trilled, "That's it!"

I stared at the stranger in the mirror. Where was the lower half of me? Hiding beneath a thousand layers of white organdy embroidered with silver threads. And where was the definition of my breasts, my best feature? Lost under a battalion of silver bugle beads marching insolently across my bust. The saleslady stuffed my arms into over-the-elbow doeskin gloves. Also required.

"Where's the groom?" I muttered. "This whole thing is getting way too serious."

"Don't be difficult," Mother snapped.

When we got home, she rushed to the phone to describe the dresses to her best friend. I had to admit the dresses were actually quite gorgeous. Father arrived at six o'clock sharp, and Mother and I placed dinner on the table instantly. His routine. Wash up, sit down to dinner. Minus suit jacket, but still in white shirt and tie. At dinner Mother gushed forth about the latest invitation, the dresses, the shoes we'd have to buy and dye to match. She also issued my marching orders. "Tomorrow, after work you'll shop for the shoes. You can take the car downtown to facilitate your movements."

The three of us just about choked on our brisket. Even with her normal sergeant-at-arms manner, this was pompous in the extreme. John tipped his chair back so that it teetered on two legs against the wall. His head rested in the greasy circle that his brown hair had christened on the yellow wall for the past two years. He crowed with laughter. Mother turned pink and looked sheepish. Under the table, Blaze wagged his plume tail, which swished in my lap. His nose rested in John's lap at the other end of the table. John slipped him a handful of green beans. John couldn't stand green beans.

But suddenly my brother turned serious. With all the disgust a sixteen-year-old boy could muster, he burst out, "Debut, debut, debut, that's all anyone can talk about around here."

Father nodded sympathetically, already visualizing the Zita bills. Then, with a puckish glint in his eye, he "organized" the dinner plates, scraping and stacking them at the end of the table.

"Saul!" Mother groaned. Stacking was as verboten as going downtown without your white gloves. And Father knew it.

There was only one thing wrong with this picture of the debutante and her doting family: I was expected to show up at all the glorious events with a date. The situation turned dire. A war mentality settled over our house, because I didn't seem to know any boys! None who qualified, anyway. No other hostesses had fixed me up—and I couldn't expect them to. I wasn't their problem. Mother and I drafted a list of potential escorts. I called several boys I'd known in high school and was rewarded with excuses and turndowns, either from the boy or his mother. "Not available." "Away at camp." "Moved." "What did you say your name was?" Next I called a former Youth Group classmate from temple. "Ronnie" came from a well-to-do Jewish family and sounded cautiously interested. But when I told him the date of the party he said, "Oh, sorry, we're going to be at our vacation house in Acapulco. My dad likes to spend time down there at his new hobby."

"What hobby?" I asked gloomily.

"Polishing his opals."

Riiiiight. Did Ronnie really have to lie to me so outrageously? I thundered down the stairs to report his alibi to my parents.

Father laughed. "We know the family. The opal polishing is true."

Oh, jeez, I had slammed the phone down for nothing.

It wasn't enough that I had to produce dates for the parties. I also needed an escort for the Coming Out Ball itself just before Christmas. That was a must.

Miraculously, I succeeded in pulling another Youth Group name out of the hat. The boy and I had been confirmed together. He said yes, even after I told him he'd have to wear a tuxedo. "Hank Moskowitz" had a round face and pleasant, clean-cut look. He went to some California college I'd never heard of, but he was smart. Holding the phone to my ear, I flushed in triumph and relief. The hardest part was over. I had a split-second impulse to say, "Well, great, now how about taking me to the nine parties I have invitations to?" But I didn't have the nerve to appear that desperate.

I sat down at my desk with a fountain pen and a fresh box of ivory (or was it eggshell?) stationery to accept all the invitations.

Love! Laugh! Panic!

Mother was now an etiquette taskmaster who lived by Emily Post and Amy Vanderbilt. You responded to a formal invitation in writing, using the same form as the invitation itself.

> Miss Rosemary Pollack
> accepts with pleasure
> the kind invitation of . . .

That ritual was easy. But I still needed dates for the parties. Father came up with a solution. "Rosemary, what you need to do is pull guys off the street and drag them into the house. Want to go to a debut dance with me? No? Get out! Next!"

John bellowed with laughter. "Hey, Rosemary, when you get a date you can wear Mom's mink stole." To make his point, he scooped up all sixty pounds of Blaze and draped the dog around his neck.

Mother scowled, then a determined look crossed her face. "I'm going to make a call." She disappeared into the den. Emerging twenty minutes later, she announced, "Rosemary, you have a date for 'Sandra Randallman's' dance!"

"I do?"

Mother had turned on the charm and brazenly called a friend from her University of Wisconsin days. The two hadn't spoken since graduation. Not that they'd stopped liking each other. They'd both just gotten busy for over twenty years. But Mother knew one pivotal fact. Myra had had a baby boy.

"Yes, indeed," Mother chortled as she did a smart fox-trot around the living room. "Dan is twenty-five and available for the dance."

Nothing was too difficult to accomplish for her daughter.

Saturday night at six o'clock, the night of the first debut dance, I stood in the living room in a frothy lavender gown with tiny sleeves and scoop neck. The doorbell rang. "Dan" was about five-ten, with a blond mustache and wavy blond hair. His look was definitely not WASP Ivy League. A little too suave to be called clean-cut, and I'd never dated anyone with a mustache before. But he was quite attractive, actually, and in his navy suit, white shirt, and silver tie presentable enough for me not to be embarrassed. In the car, I found him to be an effortless talker. He had an "I've-been-around" quality to him that made me feel at ease. But also a bit wary.

Neither of us was prepared for the grandeur that greeted us at the Randallman estate. A uniformed young man ushered us to the parking lot, big enough to hold a movie theater crowd, and pointed the way to the backyard. At my house it was a backyard. Here it was a private park. We heard music, but couldn't even see the party, the tree-lined driveway was so long. Japanese paper lanterns hung from the branches. We walked and walked. My lavender pumps began to rub against my toes. I tucked my white-gloved hand into the crook of Dan's arm and we arrived. Sandra's parents, whom I'd never met, smiled tentatively until I introduced myself. My name rang a legitimate bell. Polite hand-shaking. "Enjoy yourselves." Then they drifted away.

We stood rooted to the spot. Was this a movie set? Off to the left was an eight-piece orchestra and polished wood dance floor, already crowded with twirling couples, the girls a blur of expensive pastel. Carrie Walleron spotted me and waved vigorously over her date's shoulder. Stationed about half a block away was a second orchestra; somehow that music didn't overlap. We surveyed the scene. Round tables covered with floral cloths and hurricane lamps. A bar and an endless buffet table with ice sculptures. Waiters in white jackets circling about with trays of hors d'oeuvres. But the crowning glory was an oval pond illuminated with colored lights. Fountains at each end cascaded over water lilies. Gliding majestically to and fro were six white swans.

We danced. Dan led me smoothly, expertly. But on the slow numbers he slid his hand down my lower back and pressed me into his body. His hips thrust forward. I tried to back off, grateful that my dress had a stiff crinoline underneath. He pressed his cheek to mine. I had trouble breathing. My eyeballs strained to check on the other girls. Were they watching Dan and me and thinking "How disgusting"? Not exactly. Most of them had both arms locked around their dates' necks and were swaying back and forth.

The only time we were allowed to enter the mansion was to use the powder room. I joined the long line. The girl in front of me pivoted to see who was behind her.

"Hi, Allison," I offered brightly.

"Hi, Rosemary," she said, then turned her back to me. "Allison" was a towering, skinny redhead, with legs twice as long as the rest of her body. In her too-short pink dress she could have passed for a flamingo. Allison was continuing her pattern of snubbing me, even though we both went to Smith and had one class together. It wasn't that I did outrageous things to scare her. I wasn't an anarchist or rabble-rouser, and anyway, such animals didn't even exist at Smith in the Fifties. Standing in the bathroom line, in a split second, I filtered out and boiled down all the possible reasons for her to dislike me, and I was left with the unpleasant residue, the sludge. Maybe she didn't like overweight, pear-shaped girls. Or public school girls. Or Jewish girls. All of which I was. I'd never know for sure.

When I came out of the powder room, the dance was just about over. Dan seemed eager to leave. I said my thank you's and we walked—no, I hobbled—to the parking lot. Amid the sea of cars, no one else appeared to be in the immediate vicinity. Dan glanced furtively around, then pushed me up against his car. I gasped—my beautiful dress collecting dust from his dirty fender. He planted his mouth on mine. Not gently and gallantly, but too hard, too insistently. This was all too fast, too soon, the wrong place, so tacky, and what if someone saw us? And then I felt his tongue sliding along my lips, persistent, slithery. What was he doing? The sensation was horrid. I kept my lips pressed tightly together, pushed hard against his chest, and broke away, struggling for breath. Suave as ever, he merely shrugged.

During the silent drive home, my eyes fixed straight ahead, I consoled myself. He didn't have the right hair; too slicked down.

Or the right tie; too flashy and silvery. But what the hell, he got me to the dance, and I had a pretty good time anyway. Until the parking lot.

The next morning, I sat thankfully alone in the breakfast nook masticating my Wheaties, selecting and hashing over in my mind what I'd report to Mother. She was already at her desk, not writing, but sewing. The shallow middle drawer of the desk was pulled open. In it sat a plastic tackle box filled with sequins and beads. Mother was making a fuchsia felt Peter Pan collar for my gray wool dress. She sewed expertly and had created her own intricate design on one side of the collar. Now she was copying it free hand, identically, on the other side—without a pattern.

"So how was the dance?" she asked, spearing four aqua beads onto her needle.

I dwelt on the details I knew she'd relish: the fountains, the swans, the egg twist rolls stuffed with filet mignon, the miniature baked Alaskas.

"So what about Dan?"

"So nothing. We won't be going out again."

Mother stitched a curlicue in metallic aqua thread. She seemed unconcerned about my future with Dan. He'd served his purpose. Carefully, she laid the jeweled collar down on the desk and looked up, her blue eyes slightly off-target so she didn't appear to be nailing me.

"I've been able to get you another date. For the Miller party."

The Millers were the beer baron family. Their daughter's invitation was to a dance at their yacht club on Pine Lake. I was curious about the dredged-up date, but I didn't want to appear too grateful. Mother would pick up on it and I'd likely end up in an arranged marriage. Considering my success rate with boys so far, maybe that wouldn't have been such a bad thing.

"So who is it?"

"Michael Malachi O'Connell. His mother's a friend of mine. The family owns a company that manufactures farm machinery. Michael's in the business too. He's twenty-four, graduated from Notre Dame."

"Sounds Irish Catholic."

Mother's full lips pursed as she pondered this. "Yes, but it's only one date."

"Thank you—I think." Actually, I was thrilled. Another date problem solved. I wondered what she'd think of my marrying a Catholic boy. If he had the right professional credentials she might have even considered it.

* * *

The minute "Michael Malachi O'Connell" set foot in our living room I liked him. He was only about five-eight, but sturdily built with big shoulders and chest. A squarish head, uncontrived brown hair, horn-rimmed glasses, and a kind face. The volume of him projected the solidity of a real person.

I flounced out the door in my blue gingham dress that showed off a newly acquired sunburn and settled in his sleek Oldsmobile. Large man, impressive car. He had the look of success about him, comfortable with money, but not *nouveau riche* glittery. Michael chatted about his afternoon. How he'd driven thirty miles to his mother's favorite bakery for fresh bread.

Driving an hour away for bread? We pulled up to the yacht club just before sunset. The crystal waters of Pine Lake showed just a slight chop and reflected the tall evergreens encircling it, the boathouses, and large homes with emerald lawns. At the yacht club marina, stately sailboats bobbed at their moorings. Halyards clinked against masts. Powerful Chris Crafts rocked side to side, itching to roar ahead.

The party took place in a ballroom overlooking the water. Michael placed his hand firmly on my back as he guided me inside. His hand felt good and right. The band was playing "Stardust" as the family warmly greeted us—Mr. and Mrs. Frederick Miller, their debutante daughter, and Fred Junior. The beauty of this family struck me. Mr. Miller, deeply tanned, in a summer white tuxedo jacket, with wavy gray hair adding to his debonair appeal. His son was a twenty-one-year-old version of his father, with black hair, olive skin, and dark sexy eyes. I was unabashedly awestruck. Miller High Life Beer was a national icon. Yet even in their yacht club world, the family seemed quite unspoiled. Michael appeared comfortable in this world too. He knew most everybody. We danced, ate jumbo shrimp, and watched the sun cast its orange and purple reflections in the water as it dipped behind the horizon.

Pulling up in front of our house at 2 a.m., Michael parked under the deep shadows of a large elm. Scared and excited all at once, I sat perfectly still. He drew me into his arms and kissed me. Gently, respectfully, even when he placed his confident hand lightly on my breast. But that was all. He ushered me to the door and gave me a brief kiss on the lips. "I'll call you," he said, then departed.

I felt a glow of happiness as I stood in our silent living room, my family asleep upstairs. Blaze opened his eyes and crept out from under the buffet. He went through his post-sleep ritual of stretching and yawning, then licked my hand.

A week later, during Sunday morning breakfast, the phone rang. I ran for it, but it was for Mother, who scowled at the interruption while she was reading her favorite comic strip. Fifteen minutes later, she returned to the table with a strange expression on her face. Slowly, deliberately, she cut a slice of toast into quarters, buttered one, and covered it with jam. She held it out to Blaze; he accepted it politely without gobbling.

Avoiding my eyes, she finally spoke. "That was Michael O'Connell's mother. Big news. Michael has entered the priesthood."

My scrambled egg congealed in my mouth. I felt like throwing up. Father set his coffee cup down with a clatter. John tilted his chair onto its two back legs and fitted his head onto the grease spot on the wall. His round face lit up in a smirk, his hazel eyes full of mischief. "Hey, Rosemary, I bet you were Michael's last date before he went into the priesthood!"

I shot my brother a look of total hatred. I was three when

he was born. The day he came home from the hospital I assumed he was merely visiting; I never *dreamed* he would actually be *staying*. One afternoon a few months later, Mother put his buggy outside and left us alone. I picked up my toy shovel, dug into my sandbox, and dumped load after load of sand into the buggy, intending to bury the squalling intruder. Mother came out of the house screaming. John had waited sixteen years for his revenge, and now, on this Sunday morning, he got it.

The news about Michael hit me hard. For several days I couldn't decide whether to congratulate myself or cry.

The final party of the summer was a dance at a private club. My date was an attractive boy named Frank, actually "Franklin Hamilton III." I'd had the guts to actually call him myself. Despite his pretentious name, he'd seemed quite charming and approachable when I'd met him at other parties to which he had come stag. No girl seemed to have claimed him. He'd put me at ease on the phone, apparently accustomed to calls from girls.

Six o'clock sharp Saturday night, my family and I had arranged ourselves around the living room as if in a well-rehearsed tableau. I stood stiffly awaiting Frank in my lime-green gown, matching satin pumps, and little beaded bag. My parents sat poised in their wing chairs. John rough-housed on the carpet with Blaze.

But when Franklin Hamilton III walked in the door, I wanted to be anywhere else in the world. Or just have the chutzpah to smack him. A five-o'clock shadow covered the lower half of his face. He looked downright swarthy. Even the blue tux jacket and black pants didn't help. The collar of his white shirt looked grimy. His black hair was uncombed. Mother was polite but cool. John took one look at him and bolted up the stairs. Blaze squeezed his hulk under Father's chair and refused to come out.

Reluctantly, I followed my so-called date out to his car. Frank started the ignition and off we drove. As we sped down Lake Drive, he reached under the driver's seat and pulled out a brown paper bag. There was a bottle inside and he began swigging from it. Whiskey. A knot of misery formed in my stomach. What should I do now? Was he drunk? I didn't even know. I'd never had experience with a drunk date. I'd never even known any drunks.

Somehow we made it to the country club. The swirling couples, the colored lights, the band playing "Moonlight Serenade," the buffet, none of it lifted my feeling of dread. Frank and I danced—or something. He could barely make it through a two-step without stumbling. Carrie Walleron followed me into the ladies room. "Is everything okay?" she asked in an anxious whisper.

I ran a comb through my hair, staring straight into the mirror so my troubled, lying eyes wouldn't meet her honest blue ones. The bottled-up me just refused to uncork. My true thoughts, aching to escape, danced on my tongue like seltzer bubbles, then popped into nothingness before I could release them. Carrie gave my arm an affectionate squeeze and left the ladies room. I chose a stall, flipped the toilet seat cover down, and sat. And sat. And sat. Girls came and went. If I'd had little red shoes like Dorothy in *The Wizard of Oz*, I'd have clicked the heels together and ordered myself home. My date had no respect for me. I didn't fit in. I felt like a fraud. After ten minutes, I decided I'd call even more attention to myself if I sat there the rest of the night. I rejoined the party.

Two miserable hours later, panic hit me. The band had stopped playing. The dance floor had emptied out, and Frank was too drunk to drive. How would I get home? A tall boy I'd never seen before approached, holding his girlfriend's hand. "I'm Scott," he said without so much as a hello. "Frank's a friend of mine. You're gonna have to drive his car to your house. My date and I will follow you in my car."

I was near tears. "What are you talking about? I can't drive his car. I can't drive any car in this dress."

"You have to," this bum of a boy said. "I'll drive him home from your house. Someone will pick up his car tomorrow."

"Why can't you drive me home? Let Frank take care of himself."

"Because he can't drive, don't you get it?"

"This isn't fair, it's not my fault," I shrieked. Suddenly, I shut up. The hostess's parents and their daughter were heading toward us. I waved, shot them a sweet smile, and called out, "Thank you so much for a lovely time." Frank gave them a bloodshot look. His friend grabbed his arm and dragged him to the parking lot. My hands shook as I gripped the steering wheel. I tried to find the pedals, but my bouffant skirt kept getting in the way. In desperation I scrunched it up and tucked it under my thighs. Something expensive ripped. My satin pump felt for the gas pedal. The twenty minutes down Lake Drive lasted forever. When I finally pulled up in front of my house, Scott parked behind me and put the finishing touches to the evening. "Man-o-man, the car was weaving back and forth. I thought you were gonna have an accident."

Not "Thanks for rescuing my pal." Not "You're a good sport."

Too angry to speak, too disgusted with Franklin Hamilton III, his fancy name, and his clod friend, too disgusted with myself for even leaving the house with him, I ran up the sidewalk and inside. A string of organdy butterflies from the hem of my skirt bobbed along behind me.

Sunday morning I slept till ten-thirty, wanting to never get up, and when I looked out my bedroom window Frank's car was gone. I'd planned on not telling my parents a thing, hoping to avoid the inevitable grilling from Mother, but no such luck. Very early, she'd seen Frank's car being driven away. Miraculously, she didn't preach. Instead, she made French toast for breakfast, my favorite. Trapped, I decided to spill the whole story.

Her eyes blazed. "Why that stinker. You know, I thought he looked terribly unkempt. I ought to call his mother and give her a piece of my mind."

"Oh, for God's sake, don't!" I begged.

Father shook his head and shuddered. "I knew this whole debut business was a mistake."

* * *

Monday afternoon I returned from work to find a long white florist's box waiting for me on the kitchen table. With John and Mother looking on, I slowly lifted the cover, pulled apart the green tissue, and discovered two dozen long-stemmed roses, gorgeous scarlet buds ready to open. A small white card read: "I'm so sorry. Frank."

None of it impressed John. "I didn't like that guy. He was a real jerk."

"Well . . ." Mother attempted. "It doesn't make up for the evening, but at least it's something. I'll put them in a vase."

"Never mind, I'll do it," I said. "You go back to your writing." I waited until the den door had closed. With a great sweep, I lifted the roses out of the box, held them high over my head, and dropped them on the floor. Stomp stomp! My leather flats landed the first blows. Stomp stomp stomp stomp! I jumped up and down, smashing, crushing, flattening the velvety petals. John whooped with delight and threw himself into a wild contortion of kicking the stems and leaves. The entire kitchen lurched into the thrall of a St. Vitus dance. The globe light fixture swayed. Glassware and china rattled in the cabinets. Blaze must have thought we were celebrating something. He fetched his tennis ball and tossed it up and down in his jaws.

Mother rushed in. "For heaven's sake, kids, it's not the roses' fault."

I snorted, "They're symbolic, Mother."

The gruesome night with Frank turned out to be an omen. From then on, bad things began to happen. I don't mean the stupid debutante fiascoes. I mean really bad things.

Back at Smith, my first semester of sophomore year, I gratefully drowned myself in my classes. I itched to talk about all the debut business to "Nanette," my best friend, but couldn't bring myself to say much. I would have sounded so pretentious; she was a full-scholarship student. But I just had to tell her about Dan in the parking lot at the Randallmans'. Listening gravely at first, Nanette exploded in a cascade of giggles.

"Rosemary, he was French kissing you!"

"*That* was French kissing? Yuck!" I joined her in a fit of

laughter.

Allison continued to ignore me. Now she even had a reason. I was the one deb to arrive at a formal dance with a drunk date.

I flew home for Christmas vacation, more debut parties, and the dreaded Coming Out Ball itself, where we would be Presented to Society.

My big prop airplane landed in Milwaukee in a heavy snowstorm, just as darkness fell. Slowly guiding our car out of the airport, Father squinted and leaned forward, tightly clutching the steering wheel. Heavy wet flakes splatted against the windshield. The wipers labored. Our tire chains crunched on the packed snow. The glare of headlights from approaching cars created almost blinding optical illusions.

I expected Mother to gush with questions about school and gossip. Did I buy the white satin pumps in New York over Thanksgiving? Blah blah blah. But she sat in the front seat, gloved hands folded, strangely subdued. Finally, in a hushed voice, she turned to me and said, "A terrible thing happened at the airport this afternoon." Her voice broke as she told me. Fred Miller and Fred Junior had taken off in their company plane, with two company pilots, just a few hours earlier. They were flying up to the North Woods for a hunting trip. In near-blizzard conditions, the plane crashed on take-off, killing all four on board.

I couldn't speak. My throat felt like it was closing up. Images of the Miller family at their yacht club party swirled in my head. The gracious mother and daughter. The handsome father and son—so pleasant and welcoming, so virile-looking, so charismatic. As we passed through the industrial south side of Milwaukee, I sensed that something was missing: the familiar pungent smell of malt that always wafted from the breweries. Probably because of the snowstorm and our rolled-up windows. But I preferred to think that some supernatural force had taken over out of respect for, in mourning for, the Millers.

The deaths were front-page national news, of course, for

days and days. But despite the horrible tragedy, the debut season rolled relentlessly on. My own party, a tea for the girls and their mothers at a local WASPy club, came off with an aura of elegance, just as Mother promised. My picture appeared in the paper in my caped velvet dress. Secretly, I marveled at how Mother managed to engineer all this. She probably could have negotiated an audience with newly crowned Queen Elizabeth II or a private chat with First Lady Mamie Eisenhower had she so desired.

Near the end of the tea, I ducked into the ladies room. One of the debs, whom I knew only as "Suzanne," stood at the sink pumping soap into her hands. A solemn-faced blonde, she said, "Nice tea," then blurted out: "I didn't go back to school. I got married a month ago."

I wanted to say, What'd you do that for? But I didn't. "Congratulations. You must be very happy."

Suzanne looked as if she were about to cry. "You know how they say sex is so wonderful? It's not. It's nothing."

"Oh." *What should I do now? Should I say I'm sorry and maybe things will improve?* Having only recently been subjected to my first French kiss, I lacked the sophistication to press her for useful details that I could pack away in the suitcase of my brain. "Thank you for coming to my party, Suzanne," I said lamely, then hurried out to scarf down a few more petit fours.

* * *

My irrepressible mother, with her indomitable social skills, managed to negotiate one final date for me, for Carrie Walleron's dance, at their home. On their front lawn, illuminated by spotlights, stood a huge sleigh hooked up to four life-size toy-store reindeer. A jolly rent-a-Santa sat on the sleigh bench, booming "Ho-ho-ho, welcome!" Mr. Walleron greeted me at the door as I stamped snow off my boots. He gave me a hug and enthusiastically asked "Marcus," my date, friendly questions. He treated us as if we were the two most important people in the whole world at that moment, even though the two-story foyer rocked with twinkling lights, a live band, and dancing couples. That was Carter Walleron's unique—absolutely sincere—talent and temperament.

Marcus was darkly handsome, Jewish, and a head taller than I. What more could I want? But there was something odd about him. He didn't walk, he didn't dance, he undulated, like a snake about to strike. He didn't care much for me, either.

The day of the dreaded Coming Out Ball itself arrived, bitter cold, but clear. Mother had reserved a table for ten for our family—not only Aunt Lucy and Uncle Maury, who lived four blocks away, but my aunts and uncles who schlepped all the way from New York and Washington.

"What for?" I screeched. "To watch me curtsy? It's ridiculous! It's not for anything I've accomplished in my life."

But Mother would not be deterred from her mission of Arriving in Society. On the Big Night she twirled about the living room in her mother-of-the-debutante gorgeous dress. Beige satin, with dark mink edging the bodice and hem. I had to admit she looked truly young and beautiful.

Me? In my extravagant white gown, I felt like a tiered wedding cake.

The debutantes had had a rehearsal the day before, with a bunch of official mothers giving us lessons on how to curtsy properly without toppling onto our knees, and how to descend the stairs on our dates' arms without tripping and otherwise disgracing ourselves. That part I was all set for. But not for the rest.

On the Big Night, Hank Moskowitz cheerfully appeared on my doorstep in his tuxedo—fresh-scrubbed and polite. *This is going to be okay*, I decided. But when we got downtown, inside the auditorium, my heart slammed on its brakes, as if my soul were teetering on the edge of a cliff. The ballroom looked about two football fields long. Lining the perimeter were dozens of large tables occupied by parents and other judgmental grownups. *What am I doing here?*

An official coordinator lady separated us: Hank to join the escorts and me to join the debutantes. I took my alphabetical place in line. All the other girls appeared calm. I felt flushed, sweaty under my armpits, and ready to faint. *Maybe I should truly faint, like in a nineteenth-century novel. Then they'll bring me smelling salts, lead me away, and nurse me with tea and calf's-foot jelly.*

I pressed the clasp of my white beaded purse. It sprang open, and I fished out a tiny bottle of pills—very very low-dose Valium, which Father had given me. I needed something. For several weeks now, every so often when I'd gotten particularly tense, red blotches had appeared on my chest. Only for a few minutes, but very noticeable. I glanced furtively around to see whether anyone was watching. Nobody was. The air was too filled with excited whispers, rustling skirts, and the orchestra strains floating from the ballroom. I popped five pills. I wasn't supposed to take that many at one time, but I was desperate to head off major embarrassment.

Finally, the coordinator lady announced, "Quiet, please, girls, it's time!" One by one the emcee—or whatever he was—announced our names. My turn. Hank was there for me and I took his arm. "We proudly introduce Miss Rosemary Pollack." I stepped into the spotlight and curtsied. Low, gracefully, and properly. I did not trip or stumble. I smiled and smiled and smiled. As I was led off to the side, Father was waiting for me in his assigned place. The debutantes' first dance was with their fathers. Mine looked very serious, not at all relaxed. As we danced, he said, "You can take that stiff, artificial smile off your face now."

Was that what I was doing? And I thought I was handling myself so well.

The dance ended and Father handed me over to Hank, who whirled me away among the other couples. I sighed in happiness. The worst was over—I thought. Then the gallant, tactful Hank whispered in my ear: "How come you got those red blotches all over your neck and chest?"

Thanks a lot. So much for the Valium miracle drug. My face turned crimson. I wanted to disappear, preferably into the Amazon jungle.

"They're going away now," he said.

So I'd been right all along. I didn't fit in. I unbelonged. I had turned back into a Jewish Cinderella with Size 8-1/2 Wide shoes. My eyes scanned the crowd for Mother. Father was leading her around the dance floor in a waltz. She looked blissfully pleased, her mink-trimmed skirt swishing to and fro. Father always joked that he knew only one step, "the Milwaukee Drag." Actually, he danced beautifully, and so did Mother. They had even won a dance contest aboard a cruise ship. Well, at least one of us was happy that night.

At 3 a.m. Hank led me to the parking lot. I half-expected a rotting pumpkin where his car had been. He drove me home, pulling into our driveway, all the way up to the back door near the garage. I wondered why. Then I found out.

"Let's get into the back seat for a minute," he said.

I didn't understand why, but robot-like, did as he asked, fluffing my silver-threaded skirt around me on the back seat. He squeezed in beside me, threw his arms around me in a clumsy embrace, and began kissing me hard on the lips. Not at all romantically. Suddenly, he pushed me backward and climbed on top of me, on top of my dress. For just a few seconds, he rubbed his body back and forth against me, then stiffened. A few more seconds passed. "Okay," he said in a matter-of-fact voice. He climbed off me, got out of the car, and led me up to the house. That was that. We never saw each other again.

If I hadn't known a French kiss when I'd experienced one, I certainly didn't understand what the devil had just happened in the driveway that night. It was days later before I figured it out. I told no one. Not even Nanette.

* * *

At 6:30 a.m. the next morning, the strident ringing of the phone pierced our sleeping house. Who would be calling so early the morning after the Coming Out Ball? I could hear Father's muffled voice as he answered. Moments later he was up, shaving, dressing, and hurrying down the stairs.

I ran down after him in my pajamas just as he was heading out the back door. "Father, where are you going? What's happening?"

Tight-lipped, ashen, he said, "A patient needs me, dear. Go back to bed, I'll see you later."

He was gone for hours. Mother, John, and I were eating a half-hearted lunch when he finally came home. Without a word he hung up his coat and felt hat and sat down in his place at our kitchen table.

In a strained voice he said, "I've been at the Wallerons' house. Something terrible has happened." Father never cried. But his eyes filled with tears as he spoke. In the middle of the night, their doorbell rang. Evelyn answered. A man stood at the front door—Carter's former business partner. The partnership had ended a year before, under bitter circumstances. But Evelyn, with her typical kindness, invited him in. He asked for Carter. Evelyn called to her husband, who got out of bed and came to the balcony overlooking the foyer. His former partner pulled out a gun, aimed it high, and shot Carter Walleron to death.

John let out a groan of pain. He dropped to the floor, where Blaze was sleeping under the table, buried his face in the dog's neck, and sobbed.

* * *

I gratefully returned to school for the second semester of sophomore year, obsessively studying for exams. I wrote my usual voluminous letters home, and Mother wrote me back at least once a week, often twice, in her graceful, curly hand.

* * *

Sixteen months later, when I was in Europe, the wonderful letters stopped. Mother's cancer had progressed. It took her at age forty-eight. We buried her in her debut ball gown. Even in the open casket, she lay in quiet dignity and elegance.

For a long time after my debut I asked myself whether the extravaganza had been worth it. What good had come out of it for me? I got to know a couple of exceptionally nice girls and we remained friends, for a few years anyway. I failed to fulfill Mother's goal for me: to capture a rich socialite young man with a dazzling professional future. My debut did not succeed in making me a social insider.

But the deeper question remained. Why did Mother need it? She had already made a great success of her life. She grew up with a vision and a flamboyant independence. She loved her children passionately and worked nonstop to make their lives better. She became a highly respected journalist and author. She was a club woman extraordinaire, a true leader. She gave lovely dinner parties serving French cuisine. And she was married to the state's most distinguished psychoanalyst. It was Mother who encouraged Father to extend his career, to go through the rigors of eight years of psychoanalytic training—three days a week by train to Chicago—to reach the top of his profession. Father never remarried. But when he entertained, it was with all the flair he had learned from Mother over the years.

But apparently her achievements weren't enough. A prestigious, loving husband and two reasonably wonderful children weren't enough. With my debut, Mother felt she personally had Arrived. The Russian immigrant child had reached the height of social success in an important Midwestern city. After she died, I reluctantly decided that that reason alone made the debut business worthwhile for me.

One more elusive element gnawed at Mother, making her crave my debut. Despite all her achievements, she could never quite fill a certain emptiness, a nagging insecurity that she was missing out on something. An unflagging romantic, she clung to a deeply embedded yearning for recognition and drama in her life. Maybe that's why her favorite comic strip was an epic filled with castles and knights and bravery: *Prince Valiant*.

Mother at age five (foreground) with her sister Lucy and parents, Harry and Elizabeth Bragarnick, in Russia in 1913. Later that year, when they arrived at Ellis Island, they looked so prosperous that they were exempt from the routine immigrant bug spraying—even though Harry had only $68 in his pocket.

LOVE! LAUGH! PANIC!

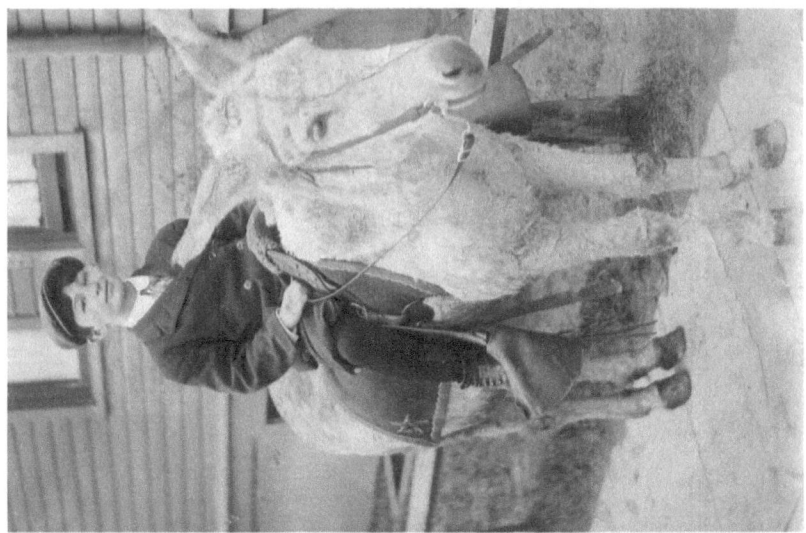

Father at fourteen.

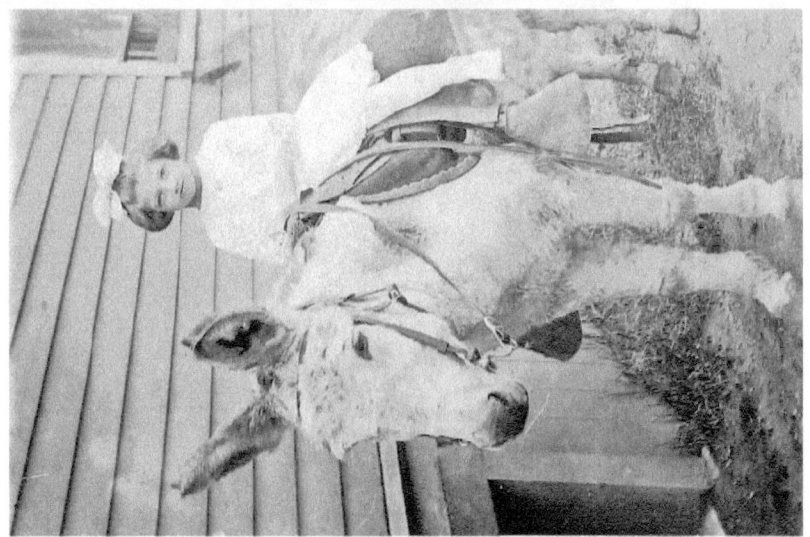

Mother at ten.

Luby and Saul's parents were best friends, so Father and Mother grew up together. Mother was four years younger.

Newlyweds Luby and Saul (the couple on the right), returning home from England in 1932.

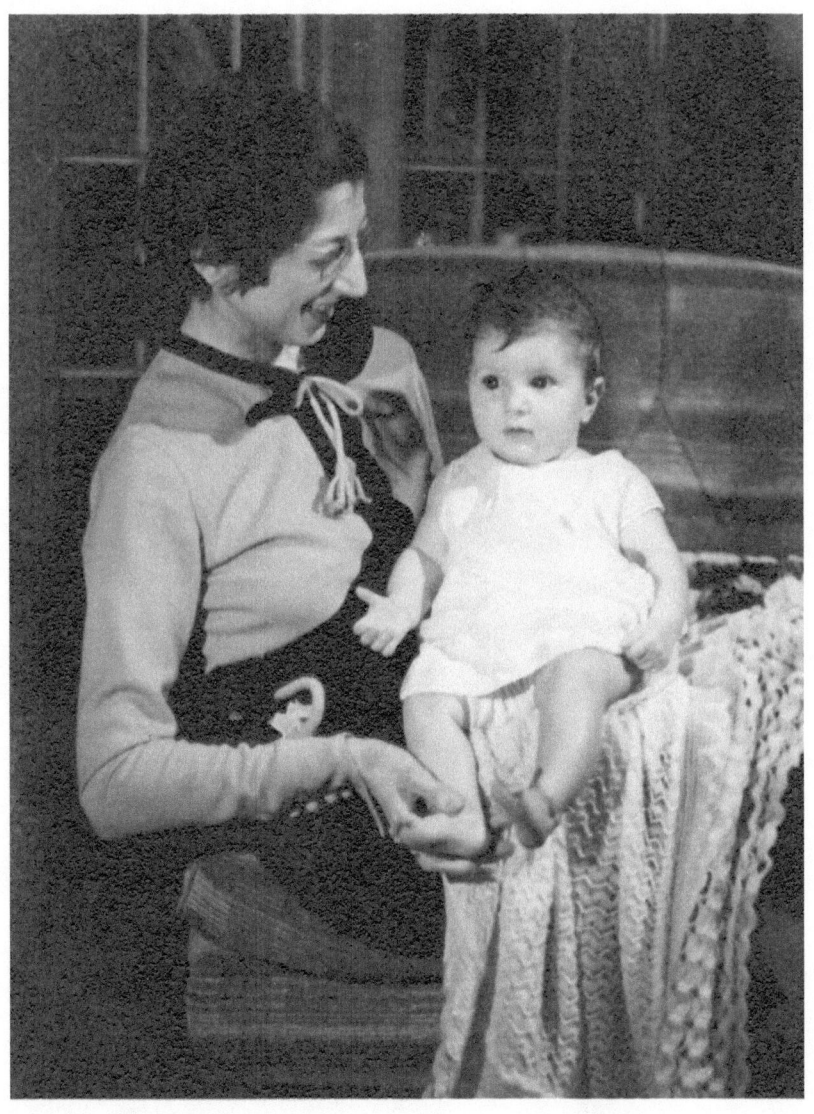

I was the first Bragarnick grandchild.
Mother called me Pussy Booboo.

Our house at 4851 North Woodburn Street, in the suburb of Whitefish Bay, Milwaukee, Wisconsin.

LOVE! LAUGH! PANIC!

Sister and brother,
John Roger Pollack and me.

Pet-sitting Curly, our friends' dog.
What a disaster. He died in our care!

Love! Laugh! Panic!

With Blaze, who was always smiling.

My parents on vacation in Cuba in 1952. Passengers had to remain on board for three days when the cruise ship arrived, because Batista was back in the country installing his military dictatorship. The politics didn't seem to be interfering with my parents' fun.

LOVE! LAUGH! PANIC!

A family dinner at the same table where Grandpa Harry held labor negotiations.

Photo by Ernest Martin-Chicago

My father's parents, Minnie and Henry Pollack, celebrate their fiftieth wedding anniversary.

Photo by the *Milwaukee Sentinel*

Grandma Elizabeth pins a flower on Grandpa Harry at his testimonial dinner. The *Sentinel* article was titled "Hundreds Pay Harry Tribute."

Grandpa Harry was Father's mentor, encouraging him to go to medical school after college. The youngest of five boys, Father was the only one to pursue higher education.

Love! Laugh! Panic!

The two Bragarnick daughters in 1928.

Debutante me, making Mother happy.

LOVE! LAUGH! PANIC!

My brother, John, in high school.

1987. Father in his garden with Rex (formally Oedipus Rex). Dr. Pollack practiced psychiatry in Milwaukee for sixty years, until nineteen days before he died on February 21, 1991.

LOVE! LAUGH! PANIC!

March 27, 2013. Larry and me, John and Ann, in Colorado Springs, Colo. Larry and I had just attended Left Coast Crime, a terrific convention for mystery writers and fans.

Also by Rosemary & Larry Mild

The Paco and Molly Mystery Series

Locks and Cream Cheese—In scandal-ridden Black Rain Corners, a Chesapeake Bay mansion harbors locked rooms and deadly secrets. A wily detective and a gourmet cook tackle the case.

Hot Grudge Sunday—Bank robbers and conspirators derail the sleuths' blissful honeymoon at the Grand Canyon. Can they nail the suspects after they themselves become targets?

Boston Scream Pie—A teenage girl's nightmare triggers a sinister tale of twins, two warring families, and a blonde bombshell who hates being called "Mom."

.

Available on Amazon.com, Kindle and Nook.

Also by Rosemary & Larry Mild

Cry Ohana, Adventure and Suspense in Hawaii—A car accident, blackmail, and murder tear apart a Hawaiian ohana (family). Danger erupts at a Filipino wedding, a Maui resort, and the Big Island's volcanic steam vents. Can the family re-unite and bring down the killer?

The Dan and Rivka Sherman Mystery Series (#1)

Death Goes Postal—Rare 15th-century typesetting artifacts journey through time, leaving a horrifying imprint in their wake. Dan and Rivka risk life and limb to locate the treasures and unmask the murderer. Not quite what they expected when they bought The Olde Victorian Bookstore.

Also by Rosemary

Miriam's World and Mine—Miriam Luby Wolfe, a junior at Syracuse U., spent her fall semester in London exploring her talents: singing, dancing, acting, and writing. But she never made it home. A terrorist bomb destroyed her plane over Lockerbie, Scotland. Learn about Miriam, the Pan Am families, the bombers, and the political fallout.

Available on Amazon.com, Kindle and Nook.

ROSEMARY MILD is an award-winning essayist and coauthor of novels and short stories with her husband, Larry. The Milds have moved from Maryland to Honolulu, Hawaii, where Magic Island is almost around the corner.

E-mail them at: roselarry@magicile.com
Visit them at: www.magicile.com

www.ingramcontent.com/pod-product-compliance
Lightning Source LLC
Chambersburg PA
CBHW020655300426
44112CB00007B/385